MW01233533

SURVIVING
FINANCIAL
DOWNSIZING
DOWNSIZING
DOWNSIZING

A Practical Guide to
Living Well on Less Income

GAIL PERRY, C.P.A.

Adams Media
Avon, Massachusetts

Published by
Adams Media, an F+W Publications Company
57 Littlefield Street, Avon, MA 02322. U.S.A.
www.adamsmedia.com

ISBN: 1-59337-017-2

Printed in the United States of America.

J I H G F E D C B A

Library of Congress Cataloging-in-Publication Data
Perry, Gail.
Surviving financial downsizing : a practical guide to living well
on less income / by Gail Perry.
p.   cm.
ISBN 1-59337-017-2
1. Finance, Personal. 2. Budgets, Personal. I. Title.
HG179.P36675 2004
332.024—dc22
2003023461

This publication is designed to provide accurate and authoritative information
with regard to the subject matter covered. It is sold with the understanding that
the publisher is not engaged in rendering legal, accounting, or other professional
advice. If legal advice or other expert assistance is required, the services of a
competent professional person should be sought.
—From a *Declaration of Principles* jointly adopted by a Committee of the
American Bar Association and a Committee of Publishers and Associations

Many of the designations used by manufacturers and sellers to distinguish
their products are claimed as trademarks. Where those designations appear
in this book and Adams Media was aware of a trademark claim, the
designations have been printed in initial capital letters.

Cover photograph by Kevin Tannenbaum/Imagestate.

This book is available at quantity discounts for bulk purchases.
For information, call 1-800-872-5627.

*This book is dedicated
to Georgia and Katherine,
with all my love.*

Contents

Acknowledgments

THIS BOOK IS a compendium of information gathered over years of study and experience. If I were to begin to list the names of all of the people who have provided training and insight into the confusing area of personal financial down-sizing, as well as all of the clients, friends, and loyal readers who have shared experiences and submitted questions that inspired the topics covered in this book, there would be little room for the book itself.

I do, however, want to include a special thank-you to Jill Alexander, my editor at Adams Media, who helped me visualize the concept for this book and saw it through to its execution, and to Susan Aufheimer and Laura MacLaughlin who provided thorough and concise editing.

Introduction

IT'S TIME FOR A CHANGE. Whether by choice or by necessity, you need to make some changes in your personal finances. You need to increase your available cash, you need to reduce your expenses, you need to make do on less—you need to take charge. Believe it or not, you can change your financial lifestyle without significantly changing your style of living. This book will show you how.

By gaining an understanding of how finances work, how money is earned, saved, and spent, and what choices you can make, you can change the way you use money without changing your level of comfort and security. You don't have to be a CPA to understand how money works in today's society. You don't have to hire one either. Instead, read what this CPA has to say; soon you'll be able to understand and take charge of your finances, and you'll eliminate many of the frightening unknowns from your financial future.

You can still plan for the future, even if the present seems financially bleak. A current setback or change in your personal finances shouldn't be used as an excuse to ignore your future plans. Use the practical information you'll find in this book to create and use your budget, meet your expenses, manage your credit, keep control of your borrowing, and keep an eye on the future, even though you experience some downsizing.

You may know in advance that you need to downsize; for example, you may be planning to retire or to stay home with children rather than work outside the home. In that case, you can use this book to help you prepare your financial plan in advance. When you have advance notice of downsizing, you can make sure your emergency fund is in place, secure your retirement money, and create a budget that will accommodate the change.

If the need to downsize comes as a surprise—an unexpected job layoff, a disability or death in the family, or a divorce—you can also use this book to help guide you through the troubled financial times. You'll find plenty of useful information that will help you protect your assets while you regroup, and you'll see how you can continue to focus on the bigger picture of your financial future even while you may face some changes in the short run.

Here's what you'll find between these covers:

Chapter 1: Where Do You Begin? Here you'll find a crash course on the various types of situations that can trigger a need for financial downsizing. You'll gain insight into where you should start if you are facing retirement, a job loss, a divorce, a disability, a death in the family, or if you've decided to cut back in order to spend more time with your family or return to school.

Chapter 2: Do You Have an Emergency Fund? Everyone needs an emergency fund—no kidding. Here's how you can start a fund, how much you need to save, and what to do if the emergency arrives before you've saved enough.

Chapter 3: Instant Savings from Expenses You No Longer Incur. If one of the wage earners in your family has lost a job, you won't like the way your income decreases, but take a look at the bright side. Having a job costs money, and you'll find lots of hidden savings and cost cutters when someone no longer has to go to work. Besides saving on transportation, meals on the job, business clothes, and other job-related expenses, you may find you save significant money on childcare, home expenses, and your food budget. And wait until you see the difference in your taxes and your insurance needs. Your income is down, but so are your expenses, so the loss may not be as great as you thought.

Chapter 4: Getting Your Share of Unemployment Benefits. Many people who are out of work qualify for unemployment benefits, money that is available from the government to help tide people over until they can get back on their financial feet. Find out if you qualify, where to start the application process, and what the rules are for how long the benefit will last. This chapter also explains how unemployment benefits are taxed, and how to appeal if you are denied benefits.

Chapter 5: Knowing Your Health Insurance Options. If you've left a job that provided health insurance benefits, you are entitled to retain those benefits for a fixed amount of time. Whether you qualify for extended health care benefits or not, there may come a time when you need to purchase health insurance on your own. This chapter explains the types of insurance, tax options relating to health insurance plans, how to shop for insurance, short-term insurance alternatives, and how to know if you're getting the best policy for the money you spend.

Chapter 6: Taking Charge of Your 401(k). Do you have a 401(k) plan? If so, you owe it to your future retired self to learn how to take the best advantage of this investment opportunity. Leaving your job doesn't mean you lose your 401(k) savings, but there are rules that must be followed if you're going to protect that money. People facing certain hardships can withdraw money from their plan without the onerous tax penalty that usually applies, but again, you have to know the rules. Are you self-employed? You can still take advantage of this special type of tax-deferred investment.

Chapter 7: Cutting Expenses: Home Economics 101. Here's one entire chapter devoted to a plethora of quick money-saving tips that can help you trim your household budget without trimming your lifestyle. Choose from tips to help you save money associated with your home, your food costs, transportation, clothing, debt and finance, entertainment, pets, and even taxes. Even if you've given a lot of thought to all the ways you can save money, there's bound to be something in this chapter you haven't tried.

Chapter 8: Budgeting Basics. Okay, here's the chapter that sounds the scariest. Most people don't like to think about budgeting and keeping track of their finances. Not only will this chapter explain how easy it is to create and maintain a budget, it will teach you how to actually use a budget to improve your lifestyle and ensure that you can afford the things you want. Make budgeting a family habit and get everyone involved. You'll all enjoy the benefits from a project you undertake together.

Chapter 9: Liquidating Assets—If Necessary. One of the reasons you make investments and acquire items of value is so that you'll have resources available to you when you need them. You may be at a time in your life when you need to cash in some of those investments in order to continue living comfortably. This chapter explains how to make careful decisions that enable you to get the most benefit from your investments while still protecting yourself in the future. Learn about the factors that contribute to the level of risk associated with your investments and how to decide when the time is right to sell shares of stock. Find out if you need life insurance and how to determine the right amount to acquire. Learn about trading one type of investment for another, and how to determine how much to withdraw from retirement plans when that time comes. This chapter also discusses the pros and cons of using assets to pay off your debts.

Chapter 10: Borrowing Money. It costs money to borrow money, but how do you know just how much it costs? This chapter provides simple explanations of the intricacies of compounded interest and the other costs of borrowing. There are benefits to borrowing money, too, such as reductions in your income tax. Learn about the pros and cons of borrowing money from a 401(k) retirement plan, and learn how to borrow money specifically targeted for those who want to pay for a college education. This chapter also includes useful information about credit ratings, how they are determined, and what factors contribute to improvement and decline in these ratings. You'll also find out information about where you can get help if your debts seem insurmountable.

Chapter 11: Taking Temporary Work. When your need for financial downsizing is temporary, taking a temporary job can add quick income to your daily cash flow while you look for something more permanent. Here are some tips on finding temporary work and getting the most benefit from temporary positions. You'll also find out how you can create your own temporary work. You don't have to wait for someone else to give you a job. Create a job of your own; it's easier than you may think.

Chapter 12: Relocating to a New Home. Use the information here to add up the financial factors you need to consider if you decide to move. Find out what it will cost you to move from one location to another and how you can maintain control of that cost. Moving costs don't end when you vacate one location; you'll have costs associated with moving into a new location as well. Learn about the hidden costs of a move, and how these costs all play out when it's time to fill out your tax returns.

Chapter 13: Enjoying the Time Off. A job loss or a decision to leave regular employment may come with financial burdens and planning issues that you need to address. But there are advantages to having some time off as well. Take the opportunity to refocus on family and friends, learn how to enjoy yourself without spending a lot of money, revitalize your hobbies, and even consider fine-tuning a hobby and turning it into a moneymaker. Get busy with repairs and other projects you've put off in the past. Consider starting a business from your home and learn about the tax considerations of such an action.

Just because you're facing some financial difficulties, you can still look forward to a secure and well-planned financial future with the information, advice, and tips in this book. Whatever questions you have about the financial obstacles you meet, the chapters in this book will help you to confront your downsizing with a positive attitude—and a positive result for you and your family.

Chapter 1

Where Do You Begin?

MANY EVENTS IN LIFE, such as the loss of a job, can cause us to rethink our standard of living and reassess how we save and spend our resources. Sometimes these events are voluntary, like choosing to have one spouse stop working in order to devote more time to the home and family. Other events catch us unaware, such as a sudden disability, or an employer's decision to reduce the size of the staff.

Maybe the unexpected will never happen, and maybe you'll always have more money than you need to meet your requirements. Or maybe not. You can wait until a life-changing event occurs and then figure out how to best deal with it, or you can anticipate the need to downsize and take comfort in your preparedness even if the worst never happens.

Whether you choose to prepare for the time when you will need to cut back, or if that time is now, this book is a useful tool for organizing the tasks necessary for meeting life's financial setbacks. You can follow along, step by step, or jump to the chapter that has the most relevance to you and your situation. Each chapter is filled with tips, advice, and guidance in making the right financial decisions for your life.

This chapter gives you a starting point in preparing for and dealing with a variety of financial setbacks, including:

- Retirement
- Unexpected job loss
- Leaving work to care for family or return to school
- Divorce
- Disability
- Death of a spouse

Retirement

One nice thing about retirement is that you usually can predict its arrival. Sooner or later most people leave the workforce. Sometimes the retirement is not voluntary, but usually you know when retirement is coming and you can take steps to plan for it.

Because it is likely you will retire eventually, there's no reason to postpone your preparation for the event. The sooner you begin preparing, the more ready you'll be when the day arrives for you to stop working. Here are some steps to point you in the right direction, no matter how far off (or close) you are to retirement.

Determine Your Goals

Retirement is a personal event and everyone has a slightly different view of how life after retirement should be. Even before you begin planning for and preparing for retirement, take the time to determine what you want to accomplish.

You can make the decision *today* to start creating a plan for achieving your goals. That doesn't mean you can't change your mind at some point in the future as your retirement gets closer. Different things are important to us at different stages of our lives, and the decisions you make about retirement at age thirty may be vastly different from the choices that appeal to you at ages fifty, sixty, and seventy. No matter what age you are, if you start your retirement planning today, you will have a path to follow—a retirement compass. With no plan, you have little incentive to begin preparing for this inevitable event.

Start by asking yourself some questions about how you see yourself when you reach what you feel is a likely retirement age. Do you want your mortgage to be paid off? Do you want to travel and explore? Do you want to offer financial help to your children or your grandchildren? Do you want a vacation home? Do you want to move to a retirement community? You can choose from many directions when thinking about your future, but any choices you make require a certain degree of financial planning. Set your goals first, then begin creating a plan.

Calculate Social Security

If you know how much money you can expect to receive from Social Security, you can use that number as a starting point for determining how much you'll need from other sources to ensure a comfortable retirement.

To find out how much you can expect in benefits, you will need to look at your Personal Earnings and Benefit Estimate Statement from the Social Security Administration. The government mails these statements to all taxpayers once a year. If you don't have your statement available, or if you would like a current one, you can fill out Form SSA-7004,

Request for Social Security Statement, and mail the form to this address:

Social Security Administration
Wilkes-Barre Data Operations Center
P.O. Box 7004
Wilkes-Barre, PA 18767-7004

You can write to the Social Security Administration and request a copy of Form SSA-7004; or you can download Form SSA-7004 by visiting the Social Security Administration Web site at *www.ssa.gov;* or, even easier, you can fill out an online request form to obtain your statement.

Analyze Your Retirement Savings

If you haven't already done so, make a worksheet summarizing all of your retirement savings accounts—how much is in each account, at what pace are they growing, and how much you currently project having when you retire.

Determine how much you will be required to withdraw and at what age, and start planning now how you're going to use that money. Will you need it to live on? Will it be enough? Even though you may be required to withdraw funds at a certain age, you may not need that money when it is withdrawn. In that case you'll want to have a plan for how to invest the retirement money you withdraw from retirement accounts.

As you get nearer to retirement, move your retirement savings accounts from more aggressive to safer investments so there is less risk that your savings will be depleted due to changes in the economy.

Health Care

Any thoughts about retirement must include plans for your health care. Medicare coverage is available for U.S.

workers who have contributed to Social Security; Medicaid is another government health program that is available for low-income retirees.

Don't leave all of your health care planning to the government. Consider joining organizations that provide group health care plans. Professional organizations offer group health plans to their members. You don't have to be a professional to join an organization that offers group benefits. The American Association of Retired Persons (AARP) offers its members a health insurance plan that supplements Medicare. You can join AARP if you are age fifty or older.

Save Your Money for Retirement

Even if you have to start small, you should begin putting money away for retirement *today!* The longer you wait, the less money you will have when you retire—it's that simple. Just look at this example. If you save $100 per month for ten years, you've stashed $12,000. If that money earns 5% over the ten years while you invest the money, you have a total of $15,529. Leave that money alone and let the interest compound for another ten years and you have a total of $25,576. After thirty years, the money has increased in value to $42,124, and after forty years the same $12,000 investment is worth $69,379. If you can earn more than 5% on your money, the return is even higher. The earlier you start saving, the longer your money will have to compound and earn more money, without you ever having to add to it. In this scenario, if you want to have $69,000 by the time you're sixty years old, and you start saving at age twenty, you need only save $100 per month for the first ten years. Wait until you're fifty years old to start saving and you would need to save $450 per month for ten years to achieve the same $69,000.

If you are employed, find out what types of retirement

savings plans are available at your workplace and take advantage of them as much as you can. If you belong to an organization or association related to your industry or profession, look into retirement plan options with that group.

Talk with your investment counselor about how much you can afford to save and how to do it. You don't have an investment counselor? Find one. Some sources for finding investment advice include the Association for Investment Management and Research (*www.aimr.com*), and the Certified Financial Planner Board of Standards (*www.cfp.net*). Another good way to find a financial planner is through a recommendation from someone you know who uses that planner. Shop around until you find an advisor you can afford who will make suggestions based on your best interest, not based on how much commission he or she earns by your investments. Look for a financial planner who charges a flat rate rather than one who makes money on commissions from sales. The money you spend today on professional advice will pay off in a more secure retirement.

The tighter your budget, the more important retirement planning becomes, because you are less likely to feel like you have extra money to tuck away for old age. It's hard to save for something that seems so far off. But if you think your economic condition is tight today, try to focus on how your life will be when your earning potential is over and you're living on the amounts you saved.

Blindsided by the Unexpected Loss of a Job

Sometimes people quit jobs on purpose, and sometimes they can predict that the end of their job is imminent. Other times, companies make downsizing decisions that seem to have nothing to do with the employees, or job performance, and everything to do with the bottom line.

If you can see the end of a job coming, you have time to prepare for the loss of income, both mentally and economically, by budgeting, saving, and considering an alternative job. If you are surprised with a sudden loss of a job, apply the same tools you would use if you were taking the time to prepare to leave your job. Keep in mind these important steps:

- Stay calm! Don't burn bridges!
- Assess your current financial situation.
- Create a game plan.
- Apply for unemployment benefits.
- Ask about future work.

Getting emotional about your sudden job loss does nothing to alleviate your problems. You can think more clearly and take logical steps to maintaining your financial security if you stay calm and approach your tasks in a rational manner.

Getting upset and lashing out against those who affected the downsizing may make you feel like you're getting even, but such a reaction probably won't help your situation. The directive to downsize may have nothing do to with you or your performance. Even if it does, you can stay in charge of your emotions and even take some steps that will benefit you in the future.

Five Things to Do Before You Leave Your Job

1. Find out what your company policy is regarding severance pay and reimbursement for unused vacations and sick days. Nothing eases the blow of leaving a job like walking out the door with a check. Sometimes severance is negotiable, so don't be afraid to ask what your company is willing to do to help ease your financial burden.

2. Ask about your retirement plan. If you participate in a company retirement plan you have options on how to deal with the money in that plan. Assuming you are at least partially vested, meaning you own the right to take the money with you, you may be able to leave the money in the plan, you may be able to roll the money over into a different type of retirement plan, or you may receive a cash distribution. There can be tax penalties associated with taking money out of a retirement plan (see Chapter 6), so get all the rules straight before you take cash from your retirement plan.

3. Ask your boss and others at your company if they can place you at another job. Corporate people often know their counterparts at similar companies. Your company may be downsizing, but your competition may be looking for people. It can't hurt to ask your boss to make a couple of calls on your behalf to try and place you in a similar job with another company.

4. Find out what type of job placement service your company is offering. Many companies offer resume and referral services to departing employees. Classes in interviewing techniques and job-search tools are also commonplace. Sometimes a company engaging in a major downsizing will bring in trainers to teach new marketable skills to employees who have lost their jobs. This can be another negotiating tool on your way out. Let your employer know you think it's fair that the company provide you with basic job search tools to help you land another job.

5. Ask for a letter of recommendation. Your employer may be willing to give you a letter to take with you when you leave; however, some employers refuse to give letters of recommendation for fear of liability issues. It can't hurt to ask, and if you get a letter, take the letter with you when you interview for new positions, or even include it in the same envelope with your resume when you respond to advertisements.

Apply for Unemployment Benefits

If you've left your job involuntarily and through no fault of your own, you may qualify for state unemployment benefits. See Chapter 4 for more information on this topic.

Assess Your Current Financial Situation

Make a list of all your liquid assets—cash, savings, stocks, mutual funds—all the money you have that's easy to access. Then list all of your existing sources of income including interest and dividend earnings, child support, alimony, rent, insurance proceeds, gifts, and so on. Now you know how much money you have and where it comes from.

Next list your regular, ongoing monthly expenses, such as house payments or rent, utilities, food, medical expenses, car payments, and insurance.

Now determine how long you can meet your monthly expenses with your current money and income. This will give

KEEP DOORS OPEN

It's not at all unusual for a company to experience a staff restructuring, only to find all of the work isn't getting done the way it once did. There might be an opportunity for you to continue doing some work for your former employer, either as a part-time employee or a contract worker hired to do one project at a time. Even if your boss isn't interested, you may have contacts in other departments who would be willing to have you do some occasional work for the company until you find another job.

you a sense of what changes need to be made in terms of increasing income or decreasing expenses. The rest of this book provides pointers on accomplishing those changes.

Create a Game Plan

You've lost a job, you know how much money and income you have, and you know how much it costs to live. Now it's time for a plan.

Your plan may include a job search, or you may go back to school. Maybe you'll move in with parents or friends. You may cash in some of your savings, sell a house, or borrow money. The steps you take may be easy or they may be difficult. The important thing, though, is to have a plan. See a goal and reach for it. Climb over the obstacles you face today on your way toward the goal you see in your future. Today's financial problems shouldn't cloud the financial security you envision for your future.

Choosing to Cut Back for Family or School

Some consider leaving work to raise a family or return to school a luxury; others consider it a necessity. However you analyze the choice, there are still a number of financial concerns to address when voluntarily leaving work. Here are four of the most important issues on which you can focus:

1. Creating a financial plan
2. How to tell your employer
3. Considering a home-based business
4. Possible tax benefits

Now let's look at each one of these topics in more detail.

Your Financial Plan—Don't Leave Work Without One!

If you take anything from this book, remember this: You *must* make a financial plan when you experience a financial downsizing. Whether you've chosen the path of downsizing or the path has chosen you, don't head down that path in the dark. Fortunately, if the decision to leave a job is your choice, you have the luxury of designing a workable financial plan *before* you experience the reduction of income.

Start with a budget. The budget is the blueprint for making all of your financial decisions, today and in the future. Chapter 8 gives you the lowdown on creating a workable budget for your family. If you're getting ready to decrease the family income, design a budget in advance and start living by the budget before you give up the extra wages. Not only does this give you practice in living on a reduced income, the difference you will save will allow you to start setting aside your emergency fund in case you encounter unbudgeted expenses.

Always remember that you can revise your budget if it turns out your income or expense expectations are wrong. Don't play catch up each month if you can't meet your budget. Find where the problems are and play fix up instead.

Telling Your Employer

The way in which you tell your employer you're going to leave your job may have long-term effects. Of course you already know how much income you'll lose by leaving your job (or switching to part-time if that is your decision). But keep an eye on the future while you're making changes today.

One day you may want to return to the job market. Take the time to discuss those long-range future plans with your employer before you walk out the company door for the last time. Make a commitment to touch base with your employer once a year. Someday you may need a referral when you decide to return to the job market, or years from now your boss may encounter a freelance or part-time opportunity that is just what you need to fill in the gaps between chauffeuring kids to school or taking classes of your own.

Leave your job on a high note and you'll have a place to start inquiring if you decide to seek employment again in the future.

Consider a Home-Based Business

If you leave your job for children or to go back to school, your hands are probably going to be full. However, you may also find that you have time to squeeze in a little work that can provide a home spending fund while you're on your hiatus from full-time employment. There are plenty of ideas for home-based businesses that can be done on either a sporadic or part-time basis.

The extra income from a home-based business can be worth a lot when you realize that you can avoid much of the cost associated with working outside the home. Chapter 3 gives you an in-depth analysis of just how much it costs to maintain a job.

The Tax Benefits of Leaving a Job

It's pretty obvious that if you reduce your income you will reduce your income taxes. But there are other tax benefits associated with reducing income that may not seem quite so obvious.

Not only is there a direct income tax reduction due to your no longer earning income, but your overall tax rate is also reduced. Because income tax rates are incremental and increase as your income increases, by reducing income you fall into a lower tax bracket. The remaining income on which you pay income tax is taxed at a lower marginal tax rate.

If you're staying home to have children, you can count on an extra exemption on your tax return for each child in your family. In 2004 exemptions are worth a $3,100 per person reduction of your taxable income.

Children also generate tax credits and additional deductions. There's a child tax credit of $1,000 per child (in 2004) for each child in your family under age seventeen. And while you will see an increase in expenses like doctors' and dentists' bills, you may also qualify for a tax deduction for some of your medical costs. Not only are your medical costs increasing, but your income is decreasing, thus increasing the amount of medical expenses you can deduct (the more money you earn, the fewer medical deductions you can claim).

Children and parents who go to school are eligible for a variety of tax credits and deductions for education expenses. Consider these: the HOPE Scholarship Credit for college freshmen and sophomores, and the Lifetime Learning Credit for anyone taking courses at a college or similar institution (see IRS Publication 970, Tax Benefits for Education, on the Internet at *www.irs.gov* for information on both); the college tuition deduction; the deduction for student loan interest; the tax-free earnings for College 529 Savings Plans and Coverdell Education Savings Accounts (see *www.savingforcollege.com* for information on both). Be sure to check with your tax advisor to see which of these items are accessible to you.

A Divorce in the Family

The financial repercussions of dealing with a divorce are among the most difficult of all family issues to discuss. Whether the divorce is amicable or nasty, the discussions about financial issues always seem to be full of tension.

Both divorcing spouses need to draw up budgets (see Chapter 8 for more information on creating budgets), and there needs to be an agreement on who is responsible for each of the expenses you once shared.

Divorces produce new expenses as well. For example, you now may be faced with having to spread your two incomes over two residences instead of one; a second vehicle; additional insurance; new furniture for the second home, along with linens, dishware, and other household necessities; increased costs for childcare; and the cost of transporting children between parents. If you can't work out the details of an effective financial plan on your own, be sure to meet with a financial advisor who can help you.

Dealing with a Disability

It's one thing to temporarily lose an income while you're out of work. It's quite another thing to lose the income from a family member who becomes disabled. If you're dealing with a disability, consider whether the disability is permanent or temporary and what type of work, if any, will be available when the disabled person is able to seek employment again. Make a list of all known options and contact a disability counselor who can help you work through the benefits and future job possibilities that are available. You can find assistance through the Disability and Business Technical Assistance Center for your region (*www.adata.org*), or call the national organization for assistance at 1-800-949-4232. You can also locate assistance through the Social Security Administration's state-by-state rehabilitation services (*www.ssa.gov*).

Determine Your Needs

When there is a disability in the family, try to consider your financial, medical, and living needs as soon as possible. In fact, it wouldn't hurt to plan ahead for the possibility that one of the family wage earners may become disabled someday. According to the Disability Statistics Center, the likelihood of experiencing a disability increases significantly with age. The following table shows disability prevalence by age group.

Age	Likelihood of disability
Under 22	1.7%
22–44	6.4%
45–54	11.5%
55–64	21.9%
65–79	27.8%
Over 80	53.5%

Source: "1994 Survey of Income and Program Participation" by Stephen H. Kaye and Paul K. Longmore, in *Disability Watch: The Status of People with Disabilities in the United States,* a report by Disability Rights Advocates, Oakland, Calif., 1997.

If you are armed with the knowledge that you can survive a disability, then you can focus on the important matters of health and care if an actual disability occurs. Here are three of the main needs you should consider:

Financial needs. Create a worksheet to determine how your financial picture has changed or is going to change. Income from the disabled worker will change, and you may encounter new expenses, such as medical care or home assistance, involved with the disability.

Medical needs. You need to know about the benefits offered by your health insurance provider and the disabled person's employer. If the person was injured on the job, there will be worker's compensation to consider. Consult with the human resources director at the disabled person's place of employment as soon as possible to find out what paperwork needs to be filed and what benefits are available. You may be required to seek medical services from particular providers or institutions.

Living needs. Depending on the type and degree of disability, you may need to hire domestic help or even move to new quarters. Don't forget to consider these types of costs when assessing your financial needs. And look into benefit coverage for these expenses. If you need to make an insurance claim you may be able to make a claim for some of these indirect costs of dealing with a disability.

Options to Consider in Returning to Work

While recovering from a disability you may want to consider alternative forms of work. Either during or after your recovery, such as it may be, you may discover you will be unable to return to the type of job you held previously. A disability counselor can guide you in learning about options for employment you may not have considered.

You may be able to use your recovery time to learn new skills that can qualify you for a different job when you are able to return to work. Here are some places to start:

- Government and community-sponsored centers for the disabled provide training, rehabilitation, and job search services. Contact your state government offices for more information.
- Computers provide great access to disabled persons for both learning new jobs and performing jobs.
- State educational agencies require schools to provide access to education for people with disabilities.
- Find disability organizations on a state-by-state basis online at *www.disabilityresources.org*.

Death and the Loss of Income

The shock of facing a death in the family can be amplified enormously by a resulting loss of family income. The last thing a family consumed with grief wants to focus on is money. There are, however, several financial factors that need to be addressed when a family faces a death.

Insurance

Did the deceased person have life insurance? Your family insurance agent can take care of everything that needs to be done to expedite the processing of life insurance proceeds. Also, check with the deceased person's employer. Many employers provide life insurance policies for employees. Often they are small policies, designed to defray the cost of a funeral.

Sometimes parents have small fully paid policies on their children, again with the thought of paying for funeral expenses. Parental policies may still be in effect, even after the children are grown and raising their own families. Check the family paperwork to see if such a policy exists.

Depending on the manner of death, there may be other insurance coverage in effect. For example, employees may be covered by an insurance policy at work if they died while on the job. Accident policies cover death caused by an accident. Auto insurance may provide death coverage if the person died in a vehicle accident. Ask your insurance agent to make sure all avenues of coverage have been explored so that the surviving family receives all the benefits to which it is entitled.

Bank and Other Accounts

If there are bank, credit union, brokerage, or retirement accounts being held in the name of the deceased person, the account institutions need to be notified of the death so that proper name changes can be made on the accounts or payments can be disbursed, depending on how the beneficiary status has been arranged.

Social Security Benefits

The Social Security Administration needs to be notified of the death. You can call the SSA at 800-772-1213. Survivors may qualify for Social Security benefits when a worker dies. A surviving spouse is eligible to receive a one-time payment from the SSA of $255 if the spouse was living with the deceased person at the time of death or, if they were not living together, if the surviving spouse is eligible for benefits according to SSA records You can read more about Social Security benefits in the event of a death in the family in the booklet, "Survivor Benefits," available online at *www.ssa.gov*, or you can request Publication 05-10084 from the SSA.

Funeral, Cards, and Calls

Another financial aspect of dealing with a death in the family is the actual cost of the funeral and interment, as well as flowers, cards of thanks, and calls to friends and other family members. Difficult as it may be to consider or even discuss these issues, the cost can be a significant drain on the family budget, especially if there is no insurance coverage. Be sure to include these costs in any budgeting and financial planning done as a result of the death of a family member.

Childcare

Immediately upon the death of a wage earner, the issue of childcare must be addressed. If there are children dependent on the deceased person, schools must be notified,

and appropriate care must be arranged. There may be a budgeting issue if a parent has died, because not only could there
be a depletion of revenue, but childcare could pose an additional expense.

Initially, family and friends are likely to assist in child-
care, but ultimately other arrangements may need to be made.

Downsizing or Changing Your Home

Another financial issue associated with a death in the
family is the possibility of a change of living arrangements. A
smaller family may require less space than previously. On the
other hand, should live-in help be required, there may be a
need for a larger home. Or there may be a reason to move in
order to be close to a child-care provider. Another reason to
consider moving might be to leave painful memories in
the past, and moving to a new home may help the family
emotionally.

If you decide to move, take advantage of the opportunity to give unneeded items to local charities such as
churches, Salvation Army, Goodwill, and so on. Keep a list of
all items donated to charity in order to be able to claim a tax
deduction.

Emotional Costs

Finally, there is a cost associated with dealing with the
emotions associated with a death in the family. Whether it's
done immediately or after some time has passed, counseling
can be beneficial to those who have lost a loved one. Adults
who lose a spouse may join a support group or purchase
books that provide inspirational reading. Schools may provide
counseling for children at little or no charge, and there are
also family counselors available to help with this type of emotional crisis.

The Bottom Line

Whatever event causes a change in household finances, the resulting confusion, frustration, anger, pain, or excitement can obscure the need for sound financial planning and taking necessary action.

The suggestions in this book help point you in the right direction for dealing with a variety of financial changes.

Chapter 2

Do You Have an
Emergency Fund?

MOST FINANCIAL ANALYSTS will tell you that you should keep an emergency fund on hand. The emergency fund is to help you when you have either an unexpected loss of income or are surprised with large, unbudgeted expenses.

Ideally an emergency fund should be comprised of cash in some sort of easily accessible interest-bearing account. The cash should represent a minimum of three months and, if possible, five to six months of your regular living expenses. Your emergency fund should have enough to cover your monthly rent or mortgage payments, car payments, minimum payments on revolving charge accounts, utilities, food, and other necessities. The point of an emergency fund is to make sure you don't suffer a change in your lifestyle while you are making a change in your life.

How Much Do You Need in Your Emergency Fund?

When considering how much money you will need to set aside for each month's worth of expenses, look beyond the income you may lose to consider other benefits that may also be lost. If one spouse loses a job that comes with benefits such as health care, life insurance, day care, and so on, these benefits may also need to be covered by an emergency fund.

If you use a financial software program such as Intuit's Quicken or Microsoft Money, you can create a report that will show you how much you spend on a monthly basis for your regular expenses. If you don't use a computer program to track your finances and you're not sure how much you spend each month on some things, start with an estimate. When you have the time, go back through your checking account for at least three months and write down how much you spent on various expenses. Then average the amounts to come up with the average monthly expenses.

See the facing page for a checklist of monthly expenses your emergency fund should be able to cover in the event of a loss of income. Some of the items on this list may not apply to you, so you can ignore them. Just be sure to fill in the amounts you do spend in a typical month, and add any other items that may not be listed here.

Note that there aren't any frills on this list: no restaurant meals, no vacations, and no entertainment expenses. The emergency fund should be used for the necessities, not the extras. It's fine if you want to save more than you need, but the purpose of this exercise is to determine just what you need.

Now that you've figured out how much you spend every month, multiply that amount by the number of months you want your emergency fund to cover. The general rule of thumb is to provide for three months if you are single and under age thirty-five, six months if you have a family or are over age thirty-five. The older you are, the longer it may take you to find a comparable job.

Expenses for a Typical Month

- ☐ Housing (mortgage, rent) $ _____
- ☐ Groceries $ _____
- ☐ Electricity/gas $ _____
- ☐ Water/sewer $ _____
- ☐ Telephone $ _____
- ☐ Cable TV $ _____
- ☐ Automobile payment $ _____
- ☐ Automobile fuel, maintenance, repairs $ _____
- ☐ Trash pickup service $ _____
- ☐ Clothing (necessities only) $ _____
- ☐ Education/day care $ _____
- ☐ Credit card payments $ _____
- ☐ Insurance $ _____
- ☐ Medical $ _____
- ☐ Church/charity $ _____

Total Monthly Expenses $ _____

Getting Started on Saving

The best way to save for an emergency fund, if you have the time, is to set aside a small amount out of each paycheck before you ever need to tap into it. Let the money build up and don't let yourself be tempted to borrow from the fund. One nice way to get a jump on an emergency fund is to deposit a tax refund or a cash gift that you receive. This is money that is not part of your regular operating budget, so you're less likely to feel the loss if you stash the money instead of spending it.

It's easy to determine how much you need to save. Actually saving the money is the hard part. If you find you need a minimum of $1,800 per month and you want to have a four-month emergency fund, you'll need to save $7,200. If you've got the time, you can put aside $200 per month for three years and you'll have your $7,200. In fact, you'll have more than that if you put your money in an interest-bearing account.

Investing Your Emergency Fund

Part of the process of contemplating how to sustain an emergency fund is deciding where to put the money in the meantime. Your emergency fund is not money you can gamble with, so don't put it into speculative investments such as stocks or stock-based mutual funds unless you are absolutely certain that your investment is safe. Also, don't tie up your money in long-term bank certificates of deposit that restrict you from touching the money for a fixed period of time. A better choice is a money market account, a mutual fund that focuses on corporate bonds, U.S. treasury bills, or even a savings account where the interest you earn may not be as high as other types of investments but where you can get to the money as quickly as you need it.

A broker can recommend safe funds for your investment. But you don't need a broker to invest in a mutual fund. You can use resources on the Internet, such as Morningstar (*www.morningstar.com*), to find out about funds. You can open your own account and send payments. Better yet, set up a direct transfer on a regular basis from your checking account or your paycheck for a painless way to invest.

You Have an Emergency, but No Emergency Fund

Where does the emergency money come from when a true emergency strikes and you have not had the time or the extra money to set aside an emergency fund? Here are seven alternatives you can explore for extra cash to help you and your family weather a financial crisis.

1. Cut your monthly expenses down to the minimum. Analyze your spending and see where you can squeeze out some extra money. Maybe you can join a car pool so you don't have to drive every day. Rent or record movies instead of going to the theater. Cook more meals at home instead of eating out. See Chapter 8 for plenty of ideas about reducing your cost of living.

2. Refinance credit cards so you are paying a lower interest rate. Many credit card companies offer new cardholders the opportunity to roll over existing credit from another card and to a lower rate. Read the details of the plan to make sure the low interest rate is not just a short-term, introductory rate, but one that will last until you pay off the balance. You may even be able to ask your current credit card company to give you a lower rate to match offers it is making to new cardholders. You can comparison shop for credit cards by making phone calls to local banks and other lenders, or by exploring resources on the Internet. Bankrate.com (*www.bankrate.com*) provides a good resource for comparison shopping. You might consider borrowing cash from a credit card, but only if you know you can pay it back soon. Credit card interest adds up too quickly to make this a good source for a loan.

3. Talk to a debt counselor. These people can help you organize and consolidate your debt so that you don't get into trouble with creditors.

4. If one spouse is still working, consider a temporary cutback in contributions to a company-sponsored retirement plan. Look at how much you are contributing and see if it makes sense to reduce the amount, just for a short period of time until you get back on your feet. However, if the employer is making a matching contribution, it would be a shame to give that up. Consider other alternatives first.

5. Quit charging! Put your credit cards away and buy only those things you can afford to pay cash for. This is not the time to get yourself deeper in debt unless there is simply no other way to get by.

6. Look into a home equity loan if you are a homeowner, or look into refinancing your mortgage at a lower interest rate. If you borrowed from a local financial institution, schedule a meeting with your mortgage lender to discuss available alternatives for refinancing. There are also Web sites that provide calculations to demonstrate how much you can borrow and how much refinancing can save you. A quick search on the Internet for "mortgage calculator" or "home equity loan calculator" will provide links to easy worksheets you can fill out online. You can then take the information to your banker to negotiate a loan, or you can even borrow money online. Most sites that contain calculators also contain links to online lenders.

7. Talk to your bank about borrowing. If you have assets you can use to collateralize a loan, you may be able to borrow cash to get you through the rough times.

Reassess Your Needs

Keep a close eye on your needs and the amounts that are available to you. If you've saved money for an emergency fund and have tucked that money away, don't just forget about it. You should reexamine your monthly financial needs regularly to make sure you still have enough saved to cover those needs. If you've added a family member, sent a child to college, or increased your monthly spending in other ways, you may need to add to your emergency fund so that you will continue to be protected.

Also, make sure your investment is sound. You may find better alternatives to the way in which you have invested your money. Make sure your money is working for you and earning interest while still remaining a safe and accessible investment.

Chapter 3

Instant Savings from Expenses You No Longer Incur

YOUR FIRST REACTION to a reduction in your income may be that your resources are dwindling. On the surface you are correct. Your income shrinks and you immediately notice you have less cash coming into your bank account than you did before. But remember, at any given time the amount of money you have at your disposal is a combination of two factors: how much income you receive and how much you spend. A quick analysis of your job-related spending will illustrate how a reduction in job income also results in a reduction in expenses.

Expenses related to your job fall into two categories. One category is the expenses directly related to your job, such as buying and maintaining a business wardrobe, eating meals while at work, and your commuting expenses. The other is the expenses that are indirectly related to your job. These are the costs you incur in the form of hiring services that you can't perform while you are at work. Examples of these expenses can include childcare, housecleaning, and restaurant food. There is a third tier of expenses related to your income that become obvious only when you analyze your complete financial picture. These expenses include taxes and insurance.

Within each of these expense categories is a variety of ways in which you can save money and time. Let's take a look at how a reduction in your income affects the specific day-to-day expenses and events in your life.

Commuting

Have you ever thought about how much it actually costs you to get to and from your job? Assuming you work outside the home, there is the obvious cost of transportation. This takes on many forms, depending on where you live and how you get from one place to another.

If, for whatever reason, you stop working, the cost of your commute disappears and the time spent commuting is now yours to put to another use. A quick analysis will show you just how much money and time is saved by no longer having to commute to your job.

Public Transportation

Public transportation costs money and it's easy to calculate exactly how much you spend on your bus, train, or subway ticket, taxi fare, or ferry fee. Beyond the cost of the ride, however, are other, subtler costs. You may incur a cost in getting to and from the place of transportation. Do you walk to the station or do you get a ride? Do you drive to the station and pay for parking? In addition to time spent getting to and from your destination, don't forget the time spent arranging your schedule so you can meet your public transportation at a designated time.

Cost doesn't just refer to money. What about the value of the time you actually spend commuting? Do you use all of your commuting time effectively? Do you prepare for the day's work, read the paper to stay up-to-date with current events, write letters to family and friends, test your skills with the daily crossword puzzle, chat with fellow commuters, or catch up on much-needed sleep? Do you use a cell phone or other hand-held communication device to stay in touch with the job while you commute? Is your time spent productively, helping you earn a living, or do you put this time to personal use?

What else is associated with commuting? Do you live in a large city where commuting can pose dangers? Do you feel you have to take off your jewelry on public transportation, lock your briefcase, and leave your electronic equipment at the office? Does commuting pose any physical danger to you? Is it necessary that you commute only in daylight hours or only on the most populated routes? These are concerns that face many commuters every day, and there may be a hidden cost involved in assuring your security.

The cost, the time, the dangers associated with commuting are all factors that contribute to your ability to get to and from your job. Give up your job and the money, time, and peace of mind is yours.

Driving Yourself to Work

Those who drive to work face other issues when they commute. The cost of commuting not only includes the cost of filling the tank, but oil, tires, fluids, and general upkeep of the car. Cars that are driven frequently have more wear and tear, so you may need to purchase a car more frequently than you would if you didn't commute to a job.

You may have to pay for parking when you arrive at your job location, and you may have to pay tolls along the way. If you carpool, you probably chip in cash for your share of the ride.

A family member who must take a car to work might leave the rest of the family without transportation, thus creating a need for a second car. If you don't get a second car, the rest of the family must rely on public transportation or the generosity of friends and neighbors to get where they need to go.

Again, there is also the cost of your time spent driving to and from work. Time spent behind the wheel is time spent focused on driving and little else. If you drive a half hour each way to go to work every day, that's five hours a week, or almost a total workday, devoted just to driving. According to the 2000 U.S. Census, the average commute time for people who work outside their home is 25.5 minutes. All that time could be used for other activities.

If you leave your job and give up your commute, you save yourself the money associated with operating your car. You may even be able to give up the car altogether, saving you a significant amount of money.

What Does Your Commute Cost?

Use the simple worksheet on the following page to determine how much you save by giving up your daily commute to work. This calculation doesn't take into account the situation where a family member has acquired an additional car for the purpose of going to and from work. If you owned a second car for work and now find you can do without the car, not only do you save all these expenses, you also save the cost of car payments, gas, oil, and maintenance for the second car.

How Much Do You Save by Not Commuting?

Cost of daily public transportation fare
(doubled for round trip): $ _____

Miles you drive, roundtrip, either to
work or to public transportation multiplied
by 37.5 cents, the 2004 standard mileage
rate determined by the federal government $ _____

Parking at your job or at a public transportation station $ _____

Tolls to and from the job $ _____

Daily carpool contribution $ _____

Daily cash out-of-pocket (total of all above
expenses) $ _____

Number of minutes spent, round trip, door
to door _____

Restaurant Meals

Most people take a break for food while working. Depending
on the time of day you work, you may take a break for break-
fast, lunch, or dinner. Some people don't eat a full meal while
working but instead eat snacks during the day, munching
while they work. Either way, there is an expense involved.

The most economical way to eat at work is to pack a
meal at home and carry it with you to your job. People who
take their meals to work won't notice a significant difference
in their meal expenses if they stop working.

Maybe you frequent the vending machines, maybe you
order out for sandwiches, or maybe you go to a restaurant
and sit down for a lunch that includes food, beverage, dessert,

and a tip for the waiter. And what about little things like a daily latte and muffin from Starbucks? At $5 or $6 (or even more) a day, the monthly expense of snacks, beverages, and full meals purchased while you're at work can really add up. Just spend one day keeping track of how much you spend on everything you put in your mouth and you'll quickly see how much money you'll save by not eating at work.

Business Wardrobe

If you wear exactly the same clothes at work that you wear at home, you're lucky. Most people have to wear business clothes, uniforms, or special work clothes, which are worn only when the time clock is running. The cost of purchasing and maintaining a business wardrobe, as well as the time spent shopping for the clothes and keeping them clean and in repair, can add up. All of this represents money and time you will save if you no longer work.

Purchasing Clothes for Your Job

Whether it's business suits and shirts and ties, wool dresses, jumpsuits, khakis, restaurant uniforms, or evening tuxes or cocktail dresses, you need clothes to wear to work. Some employers provide clothes for employees, particularly if the clothing is a specific uniform. For others, the work wardrobe represents an expense that wouldn't exist but for the job.

A work wardrobe may need replacing more frequently than the clothes you wear for comfort or housework. The clothes and accessories you wear make up your complete work wardrobe. Use the following checklist to figure out how much you spend on clothes for your job. Check off the items that apply to you, then enter the approximate amount you spend in one year of working that wouldn't be spent if you hadn't needed the items for work. This will give you a good idea of how much money you will save on clothing if you don't have a job. Work clothes can include any of the following items:

The Cost of Your Work Wardrobe

❏ Suits (matching jacket and pants or skirt) $_____

❏ Shirts or blouses $_____

❏ Ties $_____

❏ Socks $_____

❏ Shoes $_____

❏ Belts $_____

❏ Hosiery $_____

❏ Jewelry, watch $_____

❏ Hair accessories $_____

❏ Blazers $_____

❏ Dress pants $_____

❏ Skirts $_____

❏ Sweaters or sweater sets $_____

❏ Dresses $_____

❏ Company uniforms $_____

❏ Khakis or similar casual pants $_____

❏ Casual shirts $_____

❏ Trench coat $_____

❏ Dress coat $_____

❏ Makeup $_____

❏ Briefcase $_____

❏ Handbag $_____

Total cost of business wardrobe $_____

Maintaining Clothes for Your Job

In addition to buying the clothes you need for work, you must keep them clean and in good repair. This may require frequent dry cleaning, laundering, and even professional repairs if you are not deft with a needle and thread or a sewing machine. You may also need a tailor or alteration specialist to help make your clothes fit properly. Shoes need polishing and sometimes require new soles, and all of these items need replacing as they show wear. Many people keep extra clothes at work in case of emergency spills or tears. Some people wear a comfortable pair of shoes or boots to the job, then change into other footwear when they get to work.

All of these costs add up and very quickly become a major expense of a working person. The maintenance, added to the cost of clothing you calculated for your work wardrobe, is the total wardrobe cost of having a job.

Unreimbursed Job Expenses

If you work, chances are you spend money related to your job. It may be just little things, like a picture frame or flowers for your desk, or a favorite type of pen or pencil. Many employers provide all the tools employees need to do their jobs efficiently, others provide minimum tools and let employees provide the rest.

Typical expenses you might incur on behalf of your employer can include any of the following:

- Education costs and related books
- Magazine subscriptions for your profession
- Mileage expense for driving to a customer location
- Supplies or tools you want to have at your workstation

- Day planner or organizer
- Personal digital assistant (PDA)
- Computer
- Software programs
- Briefcase or other carrying case
- Professional license or license to perform certain work
- Professional dues

Childcare

If you have children, the cost of working can skyrocket. Qualified child-care providers are expensive and, depending on the type of care your child requires, you may find that you must spend an enormous portion of one spouse's take-home pay on childcare. Even parents who work part-time still incur the expense of caring for small children. Once children get to school, child-care costs diminish, but there are still costs associated with summer and holiday care as well as care when children are sick or schools are closed for various reasons.

Direct costs of childcare include fees paid to day-care providers, after-school programs, baby sitters, and nannies. If you have a worker in your home you may be required to pay taxes on behalf of the worker in addition to wages.

Indirect costs of childcare can include any of the following items:

- Transportation to and from the child-care location
- Food for a child-care provider in your home
- Gas for a child-care provider who drives your child places
- Craft and snack contributions to the child-care center
- Late pick-up charges at the child-care center
- Cost of an additional care provider if your child is sick and cannot go to a child-care center

THE HIDDEN COSTS OF CHILDCARE

In addition to the obvious money-out-the-door costs of caring for children, there are less obvious costs. Parents who work often endure a division of loyalties between job and family and this can have ramifications in terms of salary and promotions. Working parents may have less flexibility in determining their schedules at work than coworkers without children, and working parents may not want to take on added job responsibilities that can lead to advancement and possibly longer hours.

Housecleaning and Maintenance

Many people who work outside the home resort to hired services for chores like housecleaning, lawn care, painting, and simple repairs. The cost of hiring someone to do this work can really add up. According to the American Maid Service Association, the average housecleaning cost is $50 to $65. If you hire someone to perform this service weekly, the bill can run $2,500 to $3,000 per year.

Leave your job or cut back to part-time and you will have more time to devote to doing more of the housework yourself. If you have children, you can oversee their performance of chores and encourage them to help pull their weight in maintaining the home you all share.

Food at Home

The cost of food can be easily controlled by watching for sales, clipping coupons, buying in bulk, and preparing meals at home instead of eating out. The trick is having the time to do all of this effectively. You can't save money if you buy everything at retail and purchase the smallest containers so that you don't have any extra when a meal is finished.

If you decide to make a meal at home but need to purchase all the essentials right down to the salt and pepper each time you cook, you might as well go out to a restaurant because chances are you won't save much by eating at home. This is one of the reasons why families where all adults work outside the house rely so much on prepared food for their meals instead of making it themselves. Not only are the necessary ingredients not available in the cupboards, but people who work full-time every day can't always find the energy to prepare meals when they get home from work.

If you suddenly find yourself with more time at home, one of the first savings you'll notice is in the food department. Not only do you stop incurring the cost of restaurant or vending machine food purchased while away at work, you also find yourself with more time and energy that can be channeled into purchasing food at a lower cost and preparing meals at home. Chapter 7 provides more detail on how to go about trimming the budget in this department.

Working parents are likely candidates for giving their children money to purchase school lunches instead of packing lunches made from scratch. A parent with added time available to devote to meal planning and preparation is more likely to provide a nourishing lunch for the child to carry to school. Once you start preparing more family meals at home, you can use leftovers for children's lunches and you save money at school as well.

Tax Benefits

It's a basic fact that the less money you earn the less you pay in income tax. But there are subtleties in the way in which your taxes are reduced, and the amount you pay the IRS is not the only tax you can count on cutting. Here are some tax benefits you can receive if you experience a reduction of income.

Federal Income Tax

Federal income tax decreases as your income decreases. Not only is there less income to be taxed, but as your income dwindles, so does the rate at which you pay income tax. Just look at the tax rates that follow to see that income tax rates drop significantly as income goes down. The federal government takes a substantially lower percentage of your income when you make less money. Note that the following income amounts reflect only the part of your income that you pay taxes on after all deductions and exemptions have been taken. For the 2004 tax year, for example, a family of four could take $22,100 off their income from a standard deduction and four personal exemptions before beginning to pay at the 10% rate.

2004 Tax Rates for Individuals

Income	Marginal tax rate
$1–7,150	10%
$7,150–29,050	15%
$29,050–70,350	25%
$70,350–146,750	28%
$146,750–319,100	33%
over $319,100	35%

2004 Tax Rates for Married Filing Jointly and Surviving Spouses

Income	Marginal tax rate
$1–14,300	10%
$14,300–58,100	15%
$58,100–117,250	25%
$117,250–178,650	28%
$178,650–319,100	33%
over $319,100	35%

2004 Tax Rates for Married Filing Separately

Income	Marginal tax rate
$1–7,150	10%
$7,150–29,050	15%
$29,050–58,625	25%
$58,625–89,325	28%
$89,325–159,550	33%
over $159,550	35%

2004 Tax Rates for Heads of Household

Income	Marginal tax rate
$1–10,200	10%
$10,200–38,900	15%
$38,900–100,500	25%
$100,500–162,700	28%
$162,700–319,100	33%
over $319,100	35%

If one spouse is leaving a job or cutting back on income earned, there is a ripple effect in taxes. You pay less or no tax on the first spouse's diminished earnings, because of the marginal tax rate structure for federal income taxes, and the income of the second spouse is now taxed at a lower rate. Calculate what your income tax was prior to downsizing your income, then calculate the tax now and see how much you will save.

State Income Tax

Most people pay state income tax in addition to federal income tax. (Exceptions are residents of Alaska, Florida, Nevada, South Dakota, Texas, Washington, and Wyoming, who all may have to pay higher amounts of other types of taxes, particularly property and consumption taxes.) As with the federal tax, the more income you earn, the higher your state tax is. In most states the income tax percentage rate remains the same no matter how much income you earn, but still, the total tax you pay is higher, the more income you earn. Likewise, take a cut in pay, and your state income tax decreases as well.

Insurance

Although your overall insurance costs might or might not go down if you lose or leave your job, in certain areas you may be able to obtain some savings.

First, most automobile insurance companies give a reduced rate if you do not use your car to commute to and from work. So, if you leave your job and no longer drive to and from work, notify your auto insurance agent immediately. In addition, you may have been required to carry liability or malpractice insurance for your professional work. This cost vanishes if you leave your job.

On the other hand, losing a job may have the result of causing your health insurance cost to increase. See Chapter 5 for more information about the cost of health insurance.

If you've experienced a financial setback, you may be tempted to reduce other insurance costs in order to save money in your newly tightened budget. Try to resist that temptation. Now more than ever you need the protection afforded by your insurance policies. When income is lower and every penny counts, the last thing you need is a severe illness, damage to your home, or an automobile accident not covered by your insurance.

Chapter 4

Getting Your Share of
Unemployment Benefits

IF YOU LOSE YOUR JOB as a result of a layoff or any other
form of termination that is not caused by a failure to perform
your duties, you may be eligible to receive unemployment
compensation, a form of state-provided insurance that can
tide you over until you find other work. The point of unemployment compensation is not to replace your income but to
keep you from financial distress for a short period of time
while you search for another job that is comparable to the one
you lost.

Unemployment compensation payments are administered by the state government in the state where you work
and are funded by payments made by employers both to state
and federal government agencies. In some states, employees
contribute to unemployment tax funds through tax deductions. You can find the unemployment compensation administrator for your state in the government pages of your
telephone book under the word "Unemployment."

You can also find a complete list of Internet links to
state-by-state information about unemployment programs at

the end of this chapter. Some states have applications available online, and each state provides information about the benefits available.

Who Qualifies for Unemployment Compensation?

Each state is entitled to set its own qualification rules. The specific rules for each state may be found on the Internet sites listed at the end of this chapter, or you can contact your state unemployment agency and ask it to send you information.

Here is a basic list of rules you can use to determine whether or not you can apply for unemployment compensation:

1. You must have earned at least a minimum amount in the past twelve-month period. The minimum amount is determined by the state. In Illinois, for example, you must have earned at least $1,600 in the last twelve months and you must have earnings in at least two of the past four quarters.

2. You must have worked for an employer who participates in the state unemployment compensation program. Some work, such as agricultural labor or domestic service, does not qualify for unemployment compensation.

3. You must be entirely out of work or working less than full-time.

4. You must not be at fault for losing your previous job. If you quit your job voluntarily, or if you were fired due to some form of misconduct, you do not qualify for unemployment compensation.

5. You must be able to work. If you are ill or disabled or cannot work for some other reason, you do not

qualify for unemployment compensation. (You may, however, qualify for worker's compensation—check with your employer.)

6. You must be available for work. If you are vacationing or returning to school or otherwise not available to take a job, you do not qualify for unemployment compensation.

7. You must be actively looking for a job, and you must accept a suitable job if it is offered to you. You will be asked to provide proof of your job-searching activities.

Keep in mind that you can't be required to look for a job outside your area of work expertise, nor can you be required to take a job that pays substantially less than the pay you received on your previous job.

Rules for Unemployment Eligibility

There are certain basic rules for unemployment compensation eligibility no matter where you live. In order to qualify for unemployment compensation you must have lost a job through no fault of your own. Generally, undisputed claims for unemployment compensation occur when the job separation is due to a layoff or cutback of the workforce. Claims for unemployment compensation get more complicated when an employee is charged with misconduct.

Employee misconduct that results in job loss usually, but not always, prevents an employee from collecting unemployment compensation. Employee misconduct means doing something (or not doing something) you knowingly understand is wrong and that results in your losing your job. If you can prove that you had no way of knowing your actions would result in job loss, you may still qualify for unemployment compensation. Usually there must be a pattern of misbehavior for your actions to provide just cause for your termination. Even if there is just cause for your termination due to one or more of your actions, cause for termination will not necessarily prevent you from succeeding in your claim for unemployment compensation.

Following are some examples of actions that can qualify as employee misconduct, along with descriptions of how these actions can be misinterpreted. These examples also explain the employer's requirement for proving misconduct and give you suggestions for refuting employer claims.

Unauthorized Absences

If you repeatedly miss work, come in late, leave early, take extra-long lunches or breaks, or are physically present on the job but not at your station, this can be grounds for your termination. If you have authorization from a supervisor for such absences, you should be prepared to provide some evidence of such authorization, such as memos stating an understanding that you will be late or not at your station at particular times or on particular days. Or you should contact a supervisor who is willing to testify on your behalf. If you were given reason to believe that such behavior is commonplace among employees at your professional level due to examples set by others in the company who have not been terminated, this will also serve in your defense.

Theft

There's stealing and then there's *stealing*. If you are accused of removing items from your company, or of using the supplies or services of your employer without permission, you can be terminated. On the other hand, if you can establish that you were given permission to perform such actions, that you did not, in fact, remove or use such items or services, or that it is commonplace for employees at your level to take such items or use such services without retribution, then you may argue effectively that you are entitled to receive unemployment compensation.

Lying

An employer can accuse you of being untruthful. In order to do so and effectively refute your unemployment claim, the employer should be able to prove how such behavior worked to the detriment of the company or your coworkers. Your employer should be able to offer either written or testimonial evidence of untruths you have told. In your defense, you should be able to show that the statements you are accused of making are actually true, or provide testimony of observers that you did not make such statements.

Disobeying

If you are terminated for disobedience on the job, the employer must demonstrate that you intentionally disobeyed rules or expectations that you had reason to know were in place. This may include disregarding company procedure in dealing with coworkers or customers, acting outside the authority vested in your position with the company, making statements or remarks that were damaging to the company, or making vulgar or profane remarks that are outside the normal bounds at your company. For your part, you should be prepared to either refute the claim that the employer is making by offering testimony from coworkers that you did not disobey company rules, or you should be able to show that you had reason to believe that you were acting within the guidelines set out for you either by rule or by the example of others in the company.

Refusing to Cooperate with Coworkers

For many jobs, cooperation with coworkers is a vital part of the position. Refusal or inability to do so may be cause for termination as long as the expectation of being able to work as a member of a team is set out at the time employment begins. If an employer can show that you are indeed unable or unwilling to cooperate with coworkers and that this is detrimental to the performance of the job, the employer may have cause for termination. The easiest way to combat such a claim is to provide testimony from coworkers that there is no problem with your ability to work productively with others. It also helps if you can prove that your work performance actually serves to benefit the company.

Lack of Qualifications to Do the Job

If an employer finds you are unqualified to do the job for which you were hired, the employer should also show that there was reason to believe you were qualified when you were hired. If indeed you are unqualified to do the job, you should show that the required qualifications were not described for you when you took the job, or that you had a reasonable expectation that training would be provided for you.

Bad Attitude

An employer may attempt to impede your claim to unemployment compensation by stating that your bad attitude is the reason for which you were terminated. The employer should be able to provide specific, documented or corroborated examples of such behavior as well as evidence of how such behavior has harmed the company or those with whom you work. You, on the other hand, should expect to prove that you were following examples of behavior that were displayed for you by others at your level working for the same company, or you should be able to bring testimony or documentation from coworkers and supervisors in support of your demeanor.

Personality Conflict

Perhaps the most difficult thing for an employer to justify is a claim that you were terminated due to a personality conflict. An employer has every right to terminate an employee if a personality conflict exists and it is impeding the business. But unless it is obvious that the employer had reason to believe the conflict should not have existed, such a personality conflict won't necessarily prevent you from being eligible to receive unemployment compensation.

Qualifying for Compensation When You Quit Your Job

Just because you walked away from a job and weren't fired doesn't necessarily mean you don't have the right to be paid unemployment compensation. There are many situations wherein an employee can quit a job and still qualify for unemployment compensation. Your state unemployment office will be able to offer guidance as to what constitutes reasonable cause for quitting a job and remaining eligible for unemployment benefits. Here are some examples of situations where you may be able to quit your job without losing your right to benefits.

Not Getting Paid

If your employer is not paying you for your work, or if you are entitled to overtime pay and not receiving that pay, you (very understandably) may feel you need to quit your job. If company policy is to not pay overtime (and that policy was understood by you when you took the job or when you began working overtime) or if there is a dispute over whether or not you are doing your job, there may be more on the table than your not getting paid, so your claim may be denied. If, on the other hand, your employer is not meeting the payroll because of financial distress, or you are being shortchanged for some other reason that is not your fault, then you very possibly will qualify for unemployment compensation when you leave your job.

Harassment

If you are the victim of harassment by a supervisor or coworker and you were unable to resolve the problem, your only recourse may have been to quit the job. If you have legitimate proof of the harassment, then you might qualify for unemployment compensation. Proof might include an eyewitness account or an admission by the perpetrator. If you think you are the victim of harassment, explain the type of harassment to an administrator at your workplace and ask what would constitute actual proof of the harassment.

Major Job Change

Let's say that you were hired to do a specific job and the requirements of that job have changed significantly. If this is unacceptable to you and you leave your job because of the job change, you may be able to receive unemployment compensation. Be prepared to show what your original job responsibilities included. An employee manual that includes a description of the job or an employer-prepared statement of your job responsibilities should suffice. You should also be prepared to explain why the new job responsibilities are unacceptable to you.

Unsafe Working Conditions

Employers are required to provide a safe working environment for employees. If you cannot continue to do your job due to a concern for your safety, and if you were not made aware of the working conditions before you accepted the job, then you might qualify for unemployment compensation.

Unfair Discipline

You may be able to receive unemployment compensation if you quit your job after being disciplined, demoted, skipped over for a promotion, or subjected to a similar condition at work, and you have clear evidence that you were treated unfairly. Such evidence might include substantiation that you performed all the tasks that were assigned to you, or proof that others who performed exactly as you did were not subjected to the same treatment. You will need to prove your case with documents and testimonies of fellow workers and point to specific clauses in the company disciplinary rules that apply to your situation.

Before you quit your job, if you expect to be successful in a claim for unemployment compensation, you will advance your case significantly by first meeting with your employer, describing your concerns, and giving your employer a chance to improve the situation.

Strike Participants and Unemployment Compensation

There are special rules that apply to members of unions and others who participate in or support union strikes. If you are a member of a union and your union votes to strike, you do not have the right to receive unemployment compensation benefits. Even in cases where you vote against the strike, you still must abide by the rules for union strikers.

If you are not a member of a union but participate in a strike by not crossing the picket line, you are treated as a striker for purposes of unemployment compensation claims and are thus not entitled to claim unemployment compensation.

On the other hand, if you have been laid off by your company because of a work shortage due to a union strike, but would be eligible to continue working at the company if the strike were not in force, you may be entitled to file a claim for unemployment compensation. In this case, as long as you are not a participant in the strike and do not refuse to cross picket lines yourself, you are not considered to be a member of the striking group for purposes of unemployment compensation claims.

Exceptions apply to the "no benefits for strikers" rule when it can be shown that a labor dispute is caused by the failure or refusal of the employer to conform to the provisions of state or federal law pertaining to collective bargaining, hours, wages, or other conditions of work. In these situations, employees may be eligible to receive unemployment compensation.

If Your Employer Contests Your Unemployment Benefits

The employer has a right to contest your claim for unemployment benefits and will no doubt do so if there is a chance that your claim can be denied. It costs employers money to have former employees receive benefits. Moreover, future unemployment tax rates are increased for employers who have had to honor unemployment claims from former employees. If the employer contests your claim, a hearing will be scheduled where both parties can put forth their explanations as to why or why not unemployment benefits should be awarded.

If your employer plans to contest your right to unemployment benefits, you should expect your employer to be prepared with documents and testimonies from coworkers supporting the employer's position that there was reason for your termination. If the company's employee manual clearly explains the rules that were broken, or if other employees testify that they witnessed you doing whatever it was that caused your termination, you may find it difficult to refute the employer's position.

On the other hand, even when rules are set out in the manual, if you never received a copy of the manual, or if the rules were regularly disregarded by your coworkers, the manual itself carries little weight. Employees can state that they saw you doing something, but they may not know the background or the reasons for your actions, or they may not realize you had received permission from a supervisor to behave the way you did.

An employer may have an excellent reason for your termination, if something you did was clearly banned in your workplace. Still, if you never received any notice of wrongdoing and the actions continued for some time, or if others in your same position were guilty of the same wrongdoing but were not terminated, there is a good possibility that you can still qualify for unemployment benefits. In order for an employer to prevail at a hearing, it should have taken the following steps in every instance where an employee engages in wrongdoing:

- Notify the employee in writing about what he or she has done wrong
- Discuss the situation with the employee
- Have the employee sign a statement acknowledging an understanding of the problem and a willingness to correct the situation

If the employer did not follow these steps in your case, you are more likely to be able to retain your benefits.

Unemployment benefit decisions do not favor the employer if the employer's position is based on a series of minor infractions as opposed to a single "last straw" infraction. An employer who can show a buildup to a single, identifiable—and serious—workplace impropriety is more likely to prevent an employee from receiving unemployment compensation.

How Should You Begin?

You can file a claim for unemployment compensation as early as the first working day after you were let go from your previous job. At the same time you will be asked to register for job placement services and the unemployment agency in your state will attempt to place you in a job for which you are qualified.

Before filing a claim for unemployment compensation, take the time to write down exactly what led to your termination or decision to quit. If possible, get statements from your employer, supervisor, or coworkers supporting your claims. Any documents that support your claim, such as an employment manual that spells out (or fails to spell out) company rules, time sheets showing time worked and for which you weren't paid, or memos from supervisors or coworkers commending your work will help you in preparing and proving your right to your claim.

When you go to the unemployment office to file your claim, take the following information with you:

- Social Security card or some other proof of your Social Security number

- Another form of identification, such as a driver's license or state identification card
- Notices you have received regarding your termination
- Names and addresses of your past employers and the number of days you worked for each employer for the past two years
- Official wage records for your past employers, such as pay stubs or W-2 forms, showing how much you earned
- Records of any pension payments you are receiving, such as check stubs or documentation
- Information about any part-time job you may have, including evidence of how much money you are making in the form of pay stubs or other documentation from your employer
- The name of your spouse's employer and your spouse's Social Security number
- Names and birth dates of your dependent children
- Information about your attempts to find another job such as names and telephone numbers from potential employers you contacted

Some states allow you to file your unemployment claim online or by telephone. After you file a claim, someone in the unemployment office will contact your employer to verify that the information provided in your application is correct. If your employer doesn't dispute the information, and you meet the qualifications for unemployment compensation in your state, your benefits will begin.

If your employer contests the information, the unemployment agency will set a date for a hearing and both you and your employer will present your case. You may want to hire an attorney who specializes in labor law if you plan to follow through with the dispute.

How Much and for How Long?

The amount you receive in unemployment compensation is based on a percentage of your income at your previous place of employment. Each state has a maximum amount that it pays so, depending on how much you earned at your previous job, you may reach the maximum unemployment benefit.

Once you make an application for unemployment compensation and your application is accepted, you can expect to wait two to three weeks for your benefits to begin. Once benefits begin, they will continue weekly or biweekly, depending on the state you live in, for as long as you qualify for the payments.

If you continue to be unemployed, your benefits continue for only so long. Most states set twenty-six weeks as the longest period of time during which you can receive unemployment compensation benefits. After the twenty-six-week period ends you can apply for extended benefits, which typically continue for another thirteen-week period. Some states offer an additional extended benefit period of thirteen more weeks. During periods of high unemployment, states have been known to temporarily extend the maximum number of weeks for which people are eligible to receive unemployment compensation.

PLACEMENT POSSIBILITIES

Most states require people who receive unemployment compensation to register for a placement program. The state unemployment agency will attempt to help you find work and may provide training if you need to improve basic skills. Unemployment agencies also provide vocational testing and counseling to help you find other areas of work for which you may be qualified.

Severance Pay and Unemployment Benefits

When you leave your job one of the areas you may negotiate with your employer is severance pay. Some companies have a standard formula for severance pay, such as one week of severance pay for each year of employment with the company. Or there may be a collective bargaining policy in place that describes how much severance an employee is to receive upon termination. With other companies severance is negotiable and is something you can discuss with your employer when you talk about leaving the company.

When you leave your job, the additional remuneration you receive, such as severance pay, reduces the amount you are entitled to receive for unemployment. Each state employs its own formula for adjusting unemployment benefits based on the amount and the duration of the pay you receive.

Rules on severance and unemployment compensation can get very complicated, and they can have a real effect on how much total money you are able to receive each week after losing your job. If you plan to apply for unemployment compensation, check your state's formula for allocating severance pay and other payouts. Knowing that will help you negotiate a better severance payout to maximize your unemployment benefits.

Tax Treatment of Unemployment Compensation

Unemployment compensation is subject to federal income tax. You are required to report unemployment compensation on page one of your individual income tax form. Prior to preparing your individual income tax form, you should receive a Form 1099-G, Certain Government and Qualified

State Tuition Program Payments, from the federal government showing how much unemployment compensation you received during the previous year. Typically, this is the amount you should put on your tax return. The Internal Revenue Service receives a copy of the same notice you receive and it will check your return to see that you reported your unemployment income.

If for any reason you do not receive a copy of 1099-G, you are not relieved of your responsibility to report on your federal tax return the full amount of unemployment compensation you received.

Some states tax unemployment compensation, others do not. Check the laws for your own state to determine whether or not unemployment compensation can be deducted from the income that is taxable in your state.

In some states, employees must contribute to the unemployment compensation program, and a certain amount is withheld from their wages; however, those contributions are not tax deductible. In such states, if employees receive unemployment compensation benefits, the unemployment compensation earnings are not included in taxable income until the employees' contributions have been recovered.

Repayments of Unemployment Compensation

Sometimes unemployment benefits have to be repaid. For example, if your former employer disputes the benefits and wins on appeal after you've already begun receiving benefits, you may have to repay some of the benefits you received. Or if you receive money under another federal program, such as a disaster relief program, you may have to repay unemployment compensation that duplicates the other compensation.

If you receive unemployment compensation and, in the same year, you pay back some or all of the unemployment compensation, you should report only the net amount received as your income from unemployment on your tax return, not the entire amount received. Put a notation on your tax return showing your computation.

If you receive unemployment compensation in one year and include that amount on your income tax return, then in the next year you repay some or all of the unemployment compensation, you can take a deduction for the amount you repaid. Note, however, that you can deduct the amount you repaid only if you itemize your deductions.

The deduction for repaid unemployment compensation is a miscellaneous deduction, subject to the 2% limitation on miscellaneous deductions. In other words, only miscellaneous deductions that exceed 2% of your adjusted gross income (AGI) are allowed as a deduction. To the extent that your repaid unemployment compensation and any other miscellaneous deductions surpass 2% of your AGI, you can reduce your taxable income with the deduction.

Tax Withholding on Unemployment Compensation

You have the option of requesting that federal income tax be withheld on your unemployment compensation. If you want federal tax withheld, you must fill out Form W-4V, Voluntary Withholding Request. Fifteen percent of your unemployment compensation will be withheld if you make this request. If you don't make a request for withholding, there will be no tax withheld. You, however, are still liable for federal income tax on your unemployment compensation, and you may owe a penalty for underpayment if you did not have enough tax withheld during the year.

If you chose to have federal income tax withheld from your unemployment compensation, the amount of tax withheld will appear on your Form 1099-G. Show this withholding on your federal income tax return along with other tax with-holding you may have had from jobs. You should attach a copy of the 1099-G to your federal income tax form when you file your tax return.

When Your Unemployment Compensation Ends

If your unemployment compensation period comes to an end and you have not yet found a job, check with your state unemployment office to see if your state offers an extension of benefits. As mentioned, many states offer an extension, usually for thirteen weeks, for out-of-work people who reapply for benefits. Some states offer a second extension as well. Sometimes there are extenuating circumstances that produce opportunities for extensions of benefits. A severely depressed economy can provide a situation ripe for such an extension. Workers who were affected by the terrorist events of September 11, 2001 were entitled to an extension of time for unemployment benefits. Other situations, such as a major downsizing of the leading employer in an area, can cause states to loosen the rules for unemployment benefit periods.

While you are receiving unemployment compensation, be sure to take advantage of all job-search, placement, and training opportunities offered by your state. It is in the state's interest to provide these services in order to reduce the amount of unemployment compensation that must be paid to its out-of-work residents. You'll find much information about your state's offerings on the Web site for your state's unemployment department.

State-by-State Unemployment Compensation Web Sites

Alabama	Department of Industrial Relations *www.dir.state.al.us*
Alaska	Department of Labor and Workforce Development *www.labor.state.ak.us*
Arizona	Department of Economic Security *www.de.state.az.us*
Arkansas	Employment Security Department *www.accessarkansas.org/esd*
California	Employment Development Department *www.edd.cahwnet.gov*
Colorado	Department of Labor and Employment *www.coworkforce.com*
Connecticut	Department of Labor *www.ctdol.state.ct.us*
Delaware	Department of Labor Division of Unemployment Insurance *www.delawareworks.com*
District of Columbia	Department of Employment Services *http://does.ci.washington.dc.us*
Florida	Agency for Workforce Innovation *www.floridajobs.org*
Georgia	Department of Labor *www.dol.state.ga.us*
Hawaii	Department of Labor and Industrial Relations *http://dlir.state.hi.us*
Idaho	Department of Labor *www.labor.state.id.us*
Illinois	Department of Employment Security *www.ides.state.il.us*
Indiana	Department of Workforce Development *www.in.gov/dwd*
Iowa	Unemployment Insurance Services Division *www.iowaworkforce.org*
Kansas	Department of Human Resources *www.hr.state.ks.us*

Kentucky	Department for Employment Services *www.kycwd.org*
Louisiana	Department of Labor *www.ldol.state.la.us*
Maine	Bureau of Unemployment Compensation *www.state.me.us/labor*
Maryland	Office of Unemployment Insurance *www.dllr.state.md.us*
Massachusetts	Division of Employment and Training *www.detma.org*
Michigan	Bureau of Workers' and Unemployment Compensation *www.michigan.gov/bwuc*
Minnesota	Workforce Center *www.mnworkforcecenter.org*
Mississippi	Employment Security Commission *www.mesc.state.ms.us*
Missouri	Department of Labor and Industrial Relations *www.dolir.state.mo.us*
Montana	Department of Labor and Industry *http://uid.dli.state.mt.us*
Nebraska	Workforce Development *www.dol.state.ne.us*
Nevada	Department of Employment Training and Rehabilitation *http://detr.state.nv.us*
New Hampshire	Employment Security *www.nhworks.state.nh.us*
New Jersey	Department of Labor *www.nj.gov/labor*
New Mexico	Department of Labor *https://uiclaims.state.nm.us*
New York	Department of Labor *www.labor.state.ny.us*
North Carolina	Employment Security Commission *www.ncesc.com*
North Dakota	Job Service North Dakota *www.state.nd.us/jsnd*

Ohio	Department of Job and Family Services *www.state.oh.us/odjfs*
Oklahoma	Workforce Oklahoma *www.oesc.state.ok.us*
Oregon	Employment Department *http://findit.emp.state.or.us*
Pennsylvania	Department of Labor and Industry *www.dli.state.pa.us*
Rhode Island	Department of Labor and Training *www.det.state.ri.us*
South Carolina	Employment Security Commission *www.sces.org*
South Dakota	Department of Labor *www.state.sd.us/dol*
Tennessee	Department of Labor and Workforce Development *www.state.tn.us/labor-wfd*
Texas	Texas Workforce Commission *www.twc.state.tx.us*
Utah	Department of Workforce Services *http://jobs.utah.gov*
Vermont	Department of Employment and Training *www.det.state.vt.us*
Virginia	Employment Commission *www.vec.state.va.us*
Washington	Employment Security Department *www.wa.gov/esd*
West Virginia	Bureau of Employment Programs *www.state.wv.us/bep*
Wisconsin	Department of Workforce Development *www.dwd.state.wi.us*
Wyoming	Department of Employment *http://wydoe.state.wy.us*

Chapter 5

Knowing Your
Health Insurance Options

HEALTH INSURANCE IS a benefit that many employed people take for granted. If you've had health insurance provided for you by an employer, you may never have had to consider searching for and purchasing insurance on your own. You're going to be surprised at the cost of health insurance when you start shopping for your own policy.

If you lose your job or change to a job that doesn't provide health insurance, that doesn't mean you should let coverage lapse; it means you need to take charge of your health insurance yourself. Going without health insurance can be dangerous from a financial as well as a health-related standpoint—one trip to the emergency room or a catastrophic illness can end up costing tens of thousands of dollars.

In this chapter you'll learn about how you should go about investigating and acquiring health insurance coverage for yourself and, if applicable, your family.

Keeping Your Coverage Through COBRA

If you were insured at work and then left your job (other than under circumstances of gross misconduct) or suffered a cutback in hours that disqualifies you for participation in your company's group health insurance plan, you are entitled to participate in the Consolidated Omnibus Reconciliation Act, otherwise known as COBRA.

COBRA is a federal program designed to help employees maintain their health insurance coverage while looking for another job or another insurer. Nearly all employees who participate in a group health insurance plan at work qualify for COBRA when they leave their job; employees who have been fired do not qualify. Ask your employer or your company human resources person if you're not sure whether you qualify or not.

If you qualify for COBRA, then you are eligible to participate in the plan for eighteen months after leaving your current job. As a COBRA participant you pay 100% of your medical insurance costs as opposed to the lower percentage that you might have paid as an employee. If you have a family that is protected by your company health insurance, the COBRA benefits extend to your family as well.

Because you pay 100% of the COBRA health insurance instead of a reduced rate that you may have paid when you were an employee, you may find that you can do better elsewhere. Certainly COBRA is a convenient option, especially if you have existing medical conditions that you might have difficulty getting coverage for on a new policy, but it's important to explore all your options.

You have sixty days to elect COBRA health insurance coverage. The sixty days start on the day your regular health insurance coverage terminates or the day the health insurance administrator sends you a notice explaining your rights under COBRA, whichever is later.

Whether or not you elect to participate in COBRA, at some point you will need to start thinking about other insurance coverage, unless you take a job with health insurance benefits within the eighteen months that you are eligible for coverage under COBRA. You cannot extend the eighteen-month COBRA period, so you will have to consider other health insurance options once the COBRA period runs out.

What to Look for in a Health Insurance Policy

Before you begin shopping around for health insurance, consider the type of coverage you really need. In order to do this effectively, you should first assess the personal health needs of yourself and your family.

Do you and, if applicable, your family members go to the doctor frequently? Do you need prescription medicine on a regular basis? Do you plan to expand the size of your family? Do you prefer to use certain regular care providers or are you willing to go to a clinic and see whichever care provider is available? Are you interested in a health plan that provides insurance coverage every time you go to the doctor, or are you more interested in coverage just for those big emergencies? Asking yourself questions like these will help you and an insurance agent determine the best type of insurance plan for your needs while still keeping the premium payments within your budget.

Health insurance comes in three levels of coverage: basic, major medical, and disability. You can choose any or all of these coverage types when purchasing a policy for yourself and your family. In addition, there are the government

Medicare and Medicaid programs for elderly and low-income individuals respectively.

Basic Health Insurance

There are two categories of basic health insurance coverage: hospitalization and medical/surgical. *Hospitalization* coverage, unsurprisingly, provides for expenses while you are hospitalized. These expenses can include the cost of a semi-private room, nursing care, operating room expenses, x-rays and lab tests, and medications and drugs. Certain outpatient procedures, such as minor surgeries, are covered by hospitalization insurance as well. Typically, elective surgery is not covered by hospitalization insurance. *Medical/surgical* insurance covers the doctor bills associated with a hospital stay. Basic health insurance coverage is the insurance most often provided by employers.

Major Medical Insurance

Major medical insurance coverage picks up the medical insurance costs not covered by a basic policy. This might include prescription drugs, doctor visits, rehabilitation expense, blood transfusions, private nurses, and so on. Typically the policyholder is responsible for paying a certain amount of the expenses out-of-pocket, with the insurance company paying the balance. The amount you pay out-of-pocket usually goes toward a deductible amount determined by your policy. (There is more information about deductibles later in this chapter.) Usually there is a maximum amount the policy will pay.

You can choose from a variety of health plan types. Get quotes from different companies and speak with more than one insurance agent before deciding on the type of insurance that you believe is best for you.

Disability Insurance

Disability insurance provides a replacement for lost income while you are unable to work. If you are employed and injured while on the job, an employer's worker's compensation insurance will reimburse you for at least a portion of lost income. Some states have disability insurance funds that provide short-term partial wage replacement for workers who are injured off the job. For example, in California, most employees contribute to the California State Disability Insurance (SDI) through payroll deductions. Rhode Island, New Jersey, New York, and Hawaii offer similar disability insurance programs. Often employers provide a disability plan to supplement amounts paid through worker's compensation or state plans.

If you are not employed, you can look into private disability insurance policies. When shopping for a disability policy of your own, make sure you and your insurance provider agree on the definition of disability. *Disability* can be defined by some insurance providers as being unable to perform your current job, but able perform a different job. Other disability policies define disability as being unable to perform skills that enable you to obtain any sort of gainful employment. Some disability policies include coverage for the time you spend in rehabilitation. Also, find out if there is a cancellation clause in your policy and decide if this is agreeable to you.

Disability policies typically provide replacement income at a percentage of your earnings immediately before you became disabled. This percentage may be negotiable depending on the amount of insurance premium you are willing to pay. Because the amount of disability insurance is based on your earnings, the necessity of investing in disability insurance may lessen if your earnings are negligible.

For more information about disability insurance, you can

send for a free copy of *The Consumer's Guide to Disability Insurance* by writing to:

> Health Insurance Association of America
> 555 Thirteenth Street, N.W.
> Washington, DC 20004

Medicare and Medicaid

Medicare is the health insurance program administered by the federal government and offered to current and former wage earners over age sixty-five. Medicare automatically becomes available at the same time you begin receiving Social Security benefits.

There are two parts to Medicare, known as Part A and Part B. Medicare Part A, which you receive for no extra charge when you receive Social Security payments, covers hospital care. Medicare Part B, which costs extra, pays for doctor expenses, lab fees, and some medical supplies. Congress added prescription drug benefits to Medicare late in 2003. The benefits will be available starting in 2006.

For more information about Medicare, you can send for a free copy of the *Medicare Handbook* by writing to:

> Health Care Financing Administration
> Publications, N1-26-27
> 7511 Security Blvd.
> Baltimore, MD 21244

Low-income people who cannot afford insurance may qualify for Medicaid. This federal program is managed by state governments, and decisions about who qualifies and how much insurance coverage they receive is made at the state level. Your state Medicaid office can provide you with more information about your options for participating in this program.

Types of Insurance Plans

When shopping for health insurance, know your alternatives. There are three types of health insurance plans available. Each has its advantages and disadvantages, depending on the type of coverage you prefer. Ask your health insurance provider for price information about all three types of plans and consider the importance of price as well as the type of services you can expect in each plan.

Fee-for-Service

A fee-for-service health plan is a plan that pays a portion of your cost for all medical services covered under the policy, without restrictions on whom you choose as a medical provider. Typically you pay for the medical services and then submit a claim to the insurance company for repayment, although some medical providers will submit the claim on your behalf.

There are two types of insurance coverage included in a fee-for-service plan, basic protection and major medical. The basic protection plan covers care for illnesses, surgery, hospital visits, and hospital expenses. The major medical plan covers preventative care expenses like checkups, prescriptions, posthospital care, and care for ongoing illnesses.

Fee-for-service plans are considered to be the most flexible type of plan because you have the freedom to choose your providers; however, you may pay more out-of-pocket for health care services than you would under the health mainte-nance organization (HMO) or preferred provider organization (PPO) plans described next.

HMO

An HMO, or health maintenance organization, provides access to health care through a group of physicians who agree to provide services under the plan. The insurance pre-miums you pay are essentially a prepayment for services. You must then go to one of the physicians in the HMO group when you need medical services. There may be a small fee for the office visit, but typically there is very little out-of-pocket expense to you when you participate in such a plan.

If you are considering an HMO, be sure to find out some information about the members of the medical group before making a commitment to that group. If you already have a family doctor and are happy with that doctor, you may not want to make a change. With an HMO you have a primary physician of your own, but your primary physician must be a member of the HMO group. Any referrals to specialists or other doctors must come from your primary physician. All prescriptions and health care must be provided by or cleared by the HMO group in order to be covered by your insurance plan. The convenience and lower cost of the physicians in the HMO group may be an enticing alternative.

The philosophy of the HMO is unique. The HMO service providers have a great incentive to keep you healthy and thus keep you from incurring high medical costs. Because regular checkups are included in the structure of the HMO fee, you are encouraged to visit a physician regularly and have small medical issues treated quickly before they become large and costly problems.

PPO

A more flexible alternative to the HMO, the preferred provider organization (PPO) enables plan participants to choose from a wider variety of physicians, hospitals, and other care providers. Unlike the HMO, where all of your care is paid for and you pay nothing out-of-pocket, a PPO requires that you share in the payment for services.

Typically you pay a reduced fee for services when you use a PPO member for your health care. All of the care providers in the PPO network agree to give a discount to PPO members and you will see this discount applied on the bills you receive from the doctor.

You are not restricted from going outside the PPO network for health care expenses and your health policy will cover expenses for care provided by non-PPO doctors. However, you won't receive a reduced rate if you use a non-PPO doctor, and your share of the expense may be greater than it would with a doctor in your PPO network.

If you use a PPO doctor, the doctor will submit the health insurance claim for you. If you use a doctor who isn't a member of the PPO network, you may have to pay the entire fee for the health care services, then file a claim with your health insurance company for a partial reimbursement.

Features of Health Insurance Plans

When shopping for a health insurance plan, you should consider the importance of features like a deductible, a co-payment or co-insurance, and a prescription drug plan. The less you have to pay out-of-pocket, beyond the amounts your insurance company covers, the more expensive your plan will be. The more responsibility you take on in the areas of deductible, co-pay, and prescription drugs, the more reasonably priced your health insurance policy will be.

Deductible Amount

Unless you purchase an HMO where you pay a flat fee and all of your medical costs are covered by the plan, you need to consider the amount of deductible that you agree to pay with your health costs.

A *deductible* is the amount you are required to pay for health care before the insurance coverage begins. Typically health insurance deductibles are annual amounts, so at the beginning of each year you start fresh, having to pay the deductible amount before you receive insurance coverage for your medical expenses.

The way the deductible works is when you incur medical expenses you pay the expenses in full up to the amount of your deductible amount. After the deductible is met, your insurance starts paying for expenses under the terms of your health plan. Say, for example, that your deductible is $500. Each time you go to the doctor you pay for your care until you've paid $500. Once you've paid $500, your insurance company starts participating in the payment of your health care expenses. The deductible may apply to your family as a whole, or there may be a deductible amount for each member of your family.

There is a direct correlation between the amount of your deductible and the amount you pay for health insurance. The higher your deductible, the lower your insurance rate. The more willing you are to take responsibility for your own medical expenses, particularly for the small, noncatastrophic illnesses, the less you can expect to pay for health insurance.

Co-Payment

Health insurance plans (other than HMOs) require a co-payment or co-insurance, a feature whereby you pay either a flat rate or a set percentage of each medical expense you incur. Usually the co-pay becomes effective after you have met your deductible. For example, if your health insurance has a $500 deductible and a $20 co-pay, you would pay the first $500 of insurable medical expenses. Then, for every medical expense after that first $500, you pay $20 and the insurance company pays the rest. In the case of co-insurance, you pay a percentage of medical costs after your deductible is met. For example, if you have an 80/20 co-insurance plan and your doctor's bill is $200, you will pay $40 of the cost, assuming your deductible has been met.

Prescription Drug Coverage

If you spend a lot of money on prescription drugs, consider looking for a prescription drug feature with your health insurance policy. There are many types of prescription drug programs. Most health insurance policies today include some type of prescription drug coverage. Sometimes that coverage is tied to a particular pharmacy and sometimes there is a reduced rate for prescriptions, no matter where you shop.

Shopping Around for Health Insurance

When you're ready to look into health insurance, don't go to the first vendor you find in the phone book and take what he or she offers. A well-organized plan of what you want will help you zero in on the best price when you start shopping for quotes.

Take Advantage of Your Medical Savings Account

If you were self-employed prior to 2004, you may have established an Archer medical savings account (MSA), which is a nice alternative to the traditional health insurance policies. An MSA is similar to an IRA (individual retirement account) in that you can make tax-deferred contributions to the account, and the earnings are also tax-deferred. Your annual contributions are limited to 65% of your health plan's deductible.

Unlike an IRA, you can withdraw MSA funds at any time, tax free, as long as you use the funds for medical expenses. Medical expenses include any items that would fall under the deductible of your medical insurance policy, as well as medical items such as eyeglasses and orthodontics, which might not be covered by insurance.

Deductible Requirements

The MSA rules require you to maintain a health insurance policy with a high deductible. For 2004, the required annual deductible amounts are $1,700 to $2,600 with maximum out-of-pocket expense of $3,450 if you are insuring just yourself, or $3,450 to $5,150 with maximum out-of-pocket expense of $6,300 if you are insuring your family. While these amounts may seem high at first glance, chances are you won't spend the entire deductible unless you have many illnesses in a year.

Putting Money into Your MSA

You are allowed to fund your MSA with a maximum of 65% of your deductible amount (75% if you have a family policy) each year. Remember, the amount you put in your MSA is tax-deferred, so you reduce your taxable income by the amount you put into your MSA account. If you don't use the entire amount in the account during the current year, the account balance carries over to the next year and future years, and the account continues to build and be available for future medical emergencies.

The only requirement regarding how often or how much (or how little) you can put into your MSA is the maximum amount described in the previous paragraph. You can set up a regular monthly payment to the account, just as you would pay your health insurance premium monthly, or you can contribute money sporadically throughout the year. You can wait until you have a medical need, then place that amount into the MSA and withdraw it immediately to pay for the medical expense.

Medical expenses that fall within your deductible can be paid with MSA funds. Typically the cost of insurance with a higher deductible is lower than health insurance policies with lower deductibles. The extra money you might have used to buy more expensive health insurance with a lower deductible goes into your account where it belongs to you—instead of the insurance provider.

Don't worry if you don't use all the funds in your MSA before the end of the calendar year. Unlike some company health plans, you don't lose the money if you don't use it. The MSA account is your account—it belongs entirely to you. You don't lose the use of the money if it isn't spent for medical expenses within a particular time limit. In fact, you don't have to spend the amounts in the account at all. You can pay your own medical expenses and let the money in your MSA build, year after year, just as you do with a retirement account. The money continues to accrue and earn interest or dividends on a tax-deferred basis. There is no tax until the money is withdrawn, and if the money is used for medical expenses, there is no tax at all.

Investing the Money in Your MSA

The MSA is an investment account and you can choose how the money is invested. Earnings on the money in your MSA grow tax-deferred and, like the other money in the account, may be withdrawn tax-free if used for medical expenses.

Because you are setting aside this money for a specific need, it isn't wise to speculate or invest in risky ventures. Your insurance agent should be able to direct you to safe investment choices that won't deplete the funds in your account.

Taking Money Out of Your MSA

You can withdraw funds from your MSA at any time; just be sure you use the funds for medical expenses. Use the funds for some other purpose and you will be subject to income tax on the withdrawal as well as a hefty 15% penalty for early withdrawal. MSA money used for medical expenses is withdrawn from the account tax-free. It's up to you to keep track of how you spend your MSA money.

When you see your doctor, buy glasses, or incur any other eligible medical expense, you can pay for the service yourself and request a reimbursement from your MSA, or you can direct the insurance agent to pay your medical provider directly.

Once you turn sixty-five, you can begin withdrawing money for any purpose from your MSA without penalty. Only amounts used for nonmedical purposes are subject to income tax at your regular tax rates. There is no dollar amount requirement for annual withdrawals after age sixty-five as there is with an IRA after age 70½; you can withdraw the money as you need it, or let it continue to grow.

The tax savings on an MSA also contribute to the value of the account. You can deduct 100% of your MSA contribution as an adjustment to income, meaning you don't have to itemize your deductions to take the deduction for the MSA contribution. Note: Current law prohibits the creation of new MSAs.

The Tax Effects of Buying Health Insurance

When you're purchasing health insurance, knowing the tax benefits that await you may help to make the high cost of insurance a bit easier to swallow. The IRS allows deductions of medical insurance for low-income taxpayers and for tax-payers who have very high medical expenses.

Some taxpayers are eligible to take the cost of health insurance and other medical costs as itemized deductions, expenses that reduce federal taxable income and thus reduce the amount of income tax you pay. Other taxpayers can take a deduction for their health insurance costs even if they don't itemize deductions. Here's how these options work and how they affect you.

Health Costs as an Itemized Deduction

Taxpayers who itemize their deductions on their tax return may qualify for a medical deduction as well. Usually, the taxpayers who itemize deductions are those who are paying a mortgage. Mortgage interest is usually the biggest tax deductible expense that people have, and it is usually all that is needed to enable you to itemize your deductions.

Claiming a deduction for medical expenses involves computing your adjusted gross income on your tax return, then multiplying that amount by 7.5%. Adjusted gross income is the total of all of your taxable income, decreased by certain amounts such as contributions to tax-deferred retirement plans, contributions to medical savings accounts, moving expenses, and interest paid on student loans. The amount of medical expenses you paid during the year that exceeds 7.5% of your adjusted gross income is the amount you are allowed to deduct as an itemized deduction.

When you add up your deductible medical expenses, you can include the following types of items:

- Birth control pills prescribed by a doctor
- Capital expenses for equipment or improvements to your home needed for medical care
- Cost and care of guide dogs or other animals aiding the blind, deaf, and disabled
- Cost of lead-based paint removal
- Expenses of an organ donor
- Eye surgery to promote the correct function of the eye
- Fertility enhancement procedures
- Hospital services fees, including lab work, therapy, nursing services, surgery
- Legal abortion
- Legal operation to prevent having children, including, for example, vasectomy and tubal ligation
- Meals and lodging provided by a hospital during medical treatment
- Medical and hospital insurance premiums
- Medical equipment including artificial limbs, false teeth, eyeglasses, contact lenses, hearing aids, crutches, and wheelchair
- Medical services fees, including doctors, dentists, surgeons, specialists, and other medical practitioners
- Oxygen and oxygen equipment
- Portion of the fee paid to a retirement home designated for medical care

- Prescription medicines (prescribed by a doctor) and insulin
- Psychiatric care at a specially equipped medical center (includes meals and lodging)
- Qualified long-term care contracts
- Special school or home for mentally or physically disabled persons
- Smoking cessation programs
- Transportation for needed medical care
- Treatment at a drug or alcohol center (includes meals and lodging)
- Wages paid to a worker who provides medical care, and the Social Security tax, Medicare tax, and unemployment tax you paid on the worker's behalf

You are not allowed to take a deduction for the following types of medical expenses:

- Bottled water
- Cost of nutritional supplements, vitamins, herbal supplements, natural medicines, and so on, unless you can only obtain them legally with a physician's prescription
- Diaper service
- Expenses for your general health, even if following a doctor's advice, including health club dues, household help, social activities such as dancing or swimming, or trips for general health improvement
- Funeral, burial, or cremation expenses
- Any illegal operation or treatment
- Life insurance or income protection policies, or policies providing payment for loss of life, limb, or sight
- Maternity clothes
- Medical insurance portion of automobile insurance

- Medicine purchased without a prescription, such as cough medicines, aspirin, and other over-the-counter drugs
- Nursing care for a healthy baby
- Surgery for purely cosmetic reasons
- Toothpaste, toiletries, or cosmetics

Source: Internal Revenue Service, Publication 17, *Your Federal Income Tax* (2002)

DON'T FALL INTO THE HEALTH INSURANCE DEDUCTION TRAP

It is a common practice for employees to have an option to pay for health insurance with pretax dollars. This is referred to as a Section 125 plan, because it is Section 125 of the Internal Revenue Code that authorizes the payment of health expenses with pretax dollars. If you pay for health insurance at work, and you use money that is not subject to income tax, you can't take a tax deduction for the health insurance. Essentially, you've already gotten the deduction by paying for the insurance with before-tax money. Deducting the insurance on your tax return would in effect give you a double deduction.

Health Insurance Deductions for the Self-Employed

Self-employed taxpayers who purchase health insurance are entitled to deduct the cost of their health insurance without having to itemize deductions. It is important to remember that the deduction is available only if you, as a self-employed taxpayer, are not eligible to participate in another health plan through your spouse's employer. Even if you decide not to participate in such a plan, you cannot take the deduction for self-employed health insurance if the plan is available to you.

If you qualify for the deduction, the amount of health insurance you may deduct cannot exceed the net income from your business—less the deduction for 50% of self-employment tax and less the deduction for a contribution to a tax-deferred retirement plan. The self-employment tax is computed on your tax schedule SE and the amount should be determined before you calculate the deduction for health insurance.

For example, let's say that a self-employed taxpayer is eligible to take a deduction for health insurance, and that taxpayer has net income of $8,000 from the business. If he or she makes a $2,000 contribution to a tax-deferred retirement plan, the health insurance deduction would be calculated in the following manner:

Net income from business:	$8,000
50% of self-employment tax from schedule SE	−612
Retirement plan contribution	−2000
Maximum health insurance deduction	$5,388

The most the taxpayer could deduct for health insurance paid during the year is $5,388. Of course, if the actual amount of health insurance payments does not exceed $5,388, the deduction is limited to the actual amount spent. The self-employed health insurance deduction is taken on page one of the tax return in the Adjustments section.

New IRS-Approved Health Reimbursement Arrangements

In 2002 the IRS ruled that employers who participate in high-deductible health care insurance policies may create health reimbursement arrangements (HRAs) with rollover rights for their employees. The rules are similar to those for an MSA. If you're employed, this is an option that may be available to you.

For an HRA to qualify for the rollover treatment, employers must provide employees with a high-deductible health insurance policy with lower premiums than the typical low-deductible health plan popular in the workplace today. In addition, employers will fund a health savings account called an HRA with money that can be used to pay for medical expenses that are not covered by the insurance plan due to the high deductible. A key factor in this plan is that employees are entitled to roll over unused HRA money from one year to the next, tax-free. Even after an employee retires or otherwise leaves a job, the money remains available for payment of medical expenses. Should the employee die, the remaining balance in the employee's HRA account is made available to the employee's spouse and dependents.

One particularly nice feature of the HRA plan is that, unlike with an MSA, the money in the account can be used to pay for health insurance premiums. The new plans are funded entirely by employers with no payroll deductions, and provide reimbursement for all types of medical expenses, including premiums for other health insurance coverage. One theory behind the new plan is that by shifting the burden of smaller, routine medical expenses to the employee, which are paid for through the employee's own HRA account, employees will be less frivolous and more cost-conscious in their decisions about using medical care services. Check with your employer to find out if your company participates in such a plan.

Where to Shop for Health Insurance

If you're ready to purchase your own health insurance, where do you start? You have several avenues that you can explore, and you should feel free to collect several price quotes before making a decision. Much of your price shopping can be done at home or at the library with the use of a computer and access to the Internet. You can also find out a lot about health insurance prices over the phone. And it never hurts to ask friends or family members who might be able to refer you to a helpful insurance agent.

Online Browsing

Start from the comfort of your personal computer by shopping for quotes online. There are some online services that enable you to explore insurance options without providing your name or committing to hearing a sales pitch from a company. This is a good way to get a feel for how much it will cost to insure you and your family. Here are some online insurance quote services. Keep in mind that the quotes you get from these services are just estimates. When an insurance company gets the actual health records of the person to be covered, the suggested premium amounts can change.

- **InsWeb at Quicken.com.** Go to *www.quicken.com,* click the Insurance Quotes option at the top of the screen, then click on Get Health Quotes for an interactive service that provides quotes from several insurers in your state based on criteria that you enter.
- **HealthInsuranceFinders.com.** Go to *www.health insurancefinders.com* and choose the type of insurance that interests you, enter some generic information such as your zip code and gender, and get quotes for free.
- **Insure.com.** Go to *www.insure.com* for free quotes on a variety of insurance types, including individual health and dental plans.

Talk to an Insurance Agent

If you already have insurance, such as automobile or homeowner's insurance, you can ask your current insurance agent for advice about health insurance. Often insurance companies give you a better rate if you purchase more than one type of insurance through the same company. If you don't have an insurance agent or want to compare prices offered at different companies, ask friends for referrals or choose from agents listed in the telephone book.

There is no charge to meet with an insurance agent to find out information about the types of policies that are offered. Prepare a list of questions for the agent before you schedule an appointment. Here are some sample questions that you can start with in forming your own list. Depending on your particular health and financial concerns, some of these questions may not be significant for you.

- What services and fees are covered and are not covered?
- What type of prescription drug coverage is available?
- What options exist for deductible limits?
- What are the prices for different types of policies?
- What HMO and PPO options are available?
- Does your insurance provider offer guidance in helping me find a plan that's right for me?
- Does the insurance provider offer a medical savings account?
- If I use care providers outside the health plan's network, what is the cost to me?
- After meeting a deductible, how much does the health plan pay in medical costs?
- Do I need a referral or an advance ruling from the health plan before seeking the services of a specialist?
- Is there an annual cap on how much I have to pay for medical expenses?

- Is there a lifetime cap on how much my policy will pay for medical expenses?
- What type of maternity, well-baby, and pediatric care does the plan cover?
- Is there a waiting period before my health policy would become effective?
- Does the policy cover home care?
- Does the plan cover physicals, mammograms, and immunizations?
- If I am considering an HMO, how many doctors participate in the program and how difficult is it to change to a different doctor if I am dissatisfied with the service I am receiving?
- With an HMO, what doctor and hospital alternatives are available if I am traveling out of town?
- If I am considering dental insurance, what types of services are covered, how much does the policy pay for different types of services, and to what extent is orthodontic work covered?
- If I am considering eye care insurance, how much does the policy pay toward eye examinations, eyeglasses, contact lenses, and how frequently does the policy allow eyeglasses and contact lenses to be replaced and still receive insurance coverage?

Associations and Professional Organizations

When examining alternatives for acquiring health insurance coverage, consider the organizations you belong to. Professional organizations often offer group health care to members, as do national fraternities and sororities, school alumni groups, credit unions, religious organizations, community groups, and many more.

If you belong to an organization, or are considering

joining an organization, ask about its group health insurance options. Advantages to participating in group health care plans include lower prices, a greater selection of benefits, and a requirement that the insurance company provide coverage to all members of the group. You can enjoy significant savings and more comprehensive insurance in a group than you can if you purchase an individual policy. If you have a preexisting medical condition, you may have difficulty getting individual coverage. With a group plan, the insurance company is required to provide coverage to you if you are a member of the group. There may be a waiting period for preexisting conditions to be covered, and some conditions may not be covered at all, but you will still be eligible to participate in the insurance plan.

Short-Term Health Coverage

If you're between jobs, on strike, a recent graduate, or waiting for an employer's health policy to become active, or without insurance coverage for any other reason, and don't expect that situation to last for a long period of time, you may want to look into a temporary health insurance plan to cover your medical expenses for a short period.

You can purchase health insurance for as short a period as one month or for as long as six months. You will probably want to consider a short-term policy as protection strictly in the event of a devastating illness or injury, although there are short-term policies available that cover all medical expenses including doctor visits and prescriptions. Because a short-term medical plan is designed to protect you from having to pay for catastrophic illness and other large medical expenses, routine examinations and preventive care are typically not covered by a short-term medical plan.

Short-term health care is more expensive than other

plans, and short-term plans allow participation for only a fixed number of months. But if you foresee a return to more regular, less expensive coverage, such plans can be a good stopgap measure.

Give Your Insurance a Checkup

Set aside some time each year to reassess your health insurance coverage. If you are employed and covered by a plan at work, there is usually an annual reassessment period when you can change your insurance options. If you purchase your own health insurance, it's up to you to schedule an annual time to look over your policy.

Consider how much you've spent in the past year on insurance premiums and on additional medical expenses. Make a complete list of all medical expenses you've incurred including prescription drugs, doctor visits, lab fees, eye care, dental services, and hospital costs. If you didn't keep track of prescription drug expenses, your pharmacy may be able to help you by printing a list of your prescription purchases for the past year. Once you've summarized all of your medical expenses, take a look at your health insurance policy to see if you're getting the health coverage you need. Ask yourself these questions when assessing your health insurance:

• **Is your health insurance policy providing coverage for the types of medical expenses you incur?** If not, look into adding other services to your policy or purchasing an additional policy or a different policy that provides the necessary coverage.

• **Are you paying a small enough amount aside from your health insurance premiums that you're not meeting**

your annual deductible? You may want to consider increasing your deductible and thus reducing your monthly premiums.

- **Is your annual deductible low enough?** If you consistently use up your entire deductible it may be cost effective to increase your premium and decrease your deductible. Estimate the cost of such a change for an entire year and determine if you would be better off with a higher premium. A switch to an HMO might be an alternative means of reducing your annual health costs.

- **Are you adding or losing any family members from your insurance?** The family requirements of your policy may need to be changed to accommodate the change in your family size.

- **Are you happy with your care providers?** If you are in an HMO, and you're not happy with the care providers, you may want to consider switching to a preferred provider or a fee-for-service health plan.

The main thing to remember when evaluating potential health insurance plans is that choosing a plan is a personal matter. The right plan for someone else is not necessarily the right plan for you. There are many options and many cost alternatives. Carefully decide what type of coverage is most important to you, then shop around to find the best policy for the best cost. Don't forget to reassess your health needs regularly and continue to look for ways to improve your health insurance coverage.

Chapter 6

Taking Charge of Your 401(k)

YOU MAY FIND YOURSELF downsizing, either temporarily or permanently, because of a job loss, an increase in family expenditures, a change in lifestyle, or any of a number of other reasons. Whether the change is long-term or short-term, you should not put your long-range retirement plans on hold. Unless your downsizing is a result of retirement, which is a completely different issue than planning for retirement, think of your retirement contributions as part of your required budgeted expenses. Don't sacrifice contributions to your retirement savings while downsizing. Chapter 7 gives you plenty of pointers for cutting expenses, but try not to skimp on the money you set aside for retirement.

One of the most popular forms of retirement saving in the workplace today is the 401(k) plan. Named for the section of the IRS Code that describes the plan, a 401(k) plan is a tax-deferred retirement plan that many employers offer to employees. Although each 401(k) plan is slightly different depending on the investment choices an employer makes and the contribution rules determined by the employer, the basic

structure of all 401(k) plans is the same. The following char-
acteristics are always present:

- **Employee contributions reduce taxable income for
the year in which they are made.** If you contribute $1,500 to
your 401(k) plan during the year, the taxable income that gets
reported to the IRS on your year-end Wage and Tax Statement
(W-2 form) will be $1,500 less than the actual wages you
earned.
- **Many employers make matching contributions.**
Although not all employers choose to make matching contributions, the option is available to all those who set up a
401(k) plan for their employees. These matching contributions are like free money provided by the employer to the
employee. Some employers match dollar for dollar what you
contribute to your plan, up to a certain limit. Other employers
match a smaller amount, such as 50 cents, 25 cents, or 10
cents for every dollar you contribute.
- **Earnings accumulate tax-deferred.** Money invested
in the 401(k) plan earns dividends, capital gain, or interest,
depending on how the money is invested. The money you
earn on your account is not subject to income tax until the
year in which it is withdrawn.
- **Money is taxed in the year it is withdrawn at your
current income tax rate.** While your 401(k) grows over the
years, the money is not taxed until you take it out, and then it's
taxed at whatever your tax rate is at the time of withdrawal.
Many retired people are taxed at a lower rate than what they
were paying at the time they made the 401(k) contributions.
- **There is an annual limit on how much you can contribute.** In 2004, the maximum anyone can contribute to an
employer-sponsored 401(k) plan is $13,000; however, tax-
payers over age fifty are entitled to contribute an additional

$3,000 for 2004. Some employers place additional restrictions on how much you can contribute. These restrictions may be based on your annual earnings or your longevity with the company.

The following chart shows the maximum contributions allowed through year 2006.

401(k) Contribution Limits

	2003	2004	2005	2006
Annual contribution limit	$12,000	$13,000	$14,000	$15,000
Over age 50, additional contribution allowed	$2,000	$3,000	$4,000	$5,000

Limits on Annual Contributions

There's more to annual contribution limits than what you see in the numbers allowed by the government. The actual amount you can contribute to an employer-sponsored 401(k) plan is a percentage of your salary, up to the annual maximum for that year. Contribution limits get complicated if your company has highly compensated individuals.

Under current law, anyone making $90,000 or more is considered to be a highly compensated individual. In order to provide some parity in benefits for wage earners who are not so high on the salary totem pole, the law limits the amount of money that highly compensated individuals can put in their 401(k) plan. Depending on the salary mix at your company, your contribution, as well as any matching contribution your employer may provide, may be limited to a percentage determined by a formula that takes into account the average percentage of a salary that the company's staff members contribute or that is contributed on their behalf. Your employer will tell you how much you are entitled to contribute, but don't be surprised if it is less than the amount allowed by the government.

Alternatives to 401(k) Contributions

For workers who want to contribute more toward their retirement than the 401(k) limits allow, there are alternatives. Don't short your retirement just because of the limits imposed by your employer's plan. When you're ready to retire or downsize for any reason and begin drawing on your retirement funds, you'll be happy to have saved as much money as possible.

Consider individual retirement accounts (IRAs) as an easy addition to 401(k) plans, and look into purchasing annuities as well. And don't forget you can save for retirement without taking advantage of the tax-deferred options. A well-rounded mix of investments in certificates of deposit, stocks, bonds, and savings will protect you as you age and also as you face unexpected expenditures.

Individual Retirement Accounts

As a 401(k) plan participant you may be ineligible to make tax-deferred contributions to IRAs, but that shouldn't stop you from creating and contributing to an IRA. You can make nondeductible contributions to an IRA, up to the maximum of $3,000 per year (for 2004), and watch the money grow tax-deferred. Even if your contribution is not tax-deductible, all the earnings in the IRA accumulate without being taxed, until such time as you begin withdrawing the money. Then the withdrawals are prorated for a tax-free and taxable portion using a formula that depends on how much you invested and how much accumulated in the account tax-deferred.

IRA options include both a traditional IRA, where tax-deferred earnings are taxed when withdrawn, and a Roth IRA, where all money grows tax-free and there is no income tax paid upon withdrawal. If you qualify for a Roth IRA and your contribution is not going to get the tax-deferral treatment due to your participation in a 401(k) plan, you may be better off setting up a Roth IRA. You can choose which type of IRA you want to use, and you can even contribute to both types in the same year. Your total annual contribution to all IRA accounts is limited to the maximum amount. For 2004, the maximum contribution is limited to $3,000. For 2005 through 2007 it will be $4,000 and in 2008 the maximum goes to $5,000. Starting in 2009 the annual maximum is scheduled to be adjusted subject to inflation. In addition, taxpayers who are at least 50 years old by the end of the year are eligible to make an extra "catch-up" IRA contribution of $500 in 2004 and 2005, $1,000 in 2006 and beyond. The maximum contribution amounts cannot exceed the taxpayer's earned income in any year.

Annuities

An annuity is like an insurance policy. You make contributions to the annuity or purchase the annuity outright for a fixed payment, and then when you retire, you begin withdrawing money from the annuity at a fixed amount each month. There are many types of annuities to consider, but some of the best provide a guaranteed fixed payment per month from the time you begin drawing money from the plan until the end of your life. The amount of the payment depends on the amount you contributed and your life expectancy at the time you begin taking payments from the plan. There are tax-deferred annuities as well as annuities that you purchase with after-tax dollars. An option discussed later in this chapter is to deposit the lump-sum proceeds from a 401(k) plan when you leave your job into an annuity. This gives you a great start on your retirement savings. You choose the financial institution that maintains the annuity and thus you have input over the way in which the money is invested.

401(k) Options When Leaving Your Job

When you leave your job you will need to make some decisions about your 401(k) plan. The plan sponsor will send you a notice about your options with regard to the plan. Included with the notice will be some forms that you can fill out and submit, indicating your choice of how you want to treat the money in your account.

Here are the types of choices you can make:

- Leave the entire amount in the plan
- Roll your entire account balance into an IRA or another employer-sponsored plan
- Take a portion of your account balance as a lump-sum payment and roll the remaining balance into an IRA or another employer-sponsored plan
- Take your entire account balance as a lump sum payment

Some plans provide you with additional options:

- Begin receiving periodic payments from the plan
- Use the account balance to purchase an annuity contract that would make monthly payments to you
- Take a portion of the account balance in a lump sum and use the remaining balance to purchase an annuity

DON'T SKIP THIS ELECTION

Beware! If you don't fill out any election forms indicating how you want to treat the money in your 401(k) account, you most likely will receive the entire balance in a lump sum payment. With the tax and penalty you will have to pay, this can be a costly decision. There is more information about getting a total payout later in this chapter.

Leave Your 401(k) Intact

If you have a balance of at least $5,000 in your 401(k) plan, you are not obliged to withdraw the money from the company plan when you leave your job. Your employer is required to let you continue to participate in the company plan if you so desire. However, your employer may require you to pay an annual maintenance fee for your continued participation, a fee the employer normally pays on behalf of current employees. This annual fee may range from about $50 to $100.

In addition, there may be an investment fee of anywhere from 0.2% to 1.5% of the money invested in the plan. You may already be paying the investment fee, as this fee is sometimes netted out of earnings before they are passed on to the fund participants. Find out if your employer plans to charge you any fees before deciding to leave your money in the plan. If you have to pay a maintenance fee, you may be better off rolling the 401(k) money into a new plan that you control.

If you do decide to leave your money intact with the company 401(k) plan, your retirement fund will continue to grow, tax-deferred, as it would if you were still an employee. You will not, however, be able to continue making contributions to the plan. Your participation in helping the plan grow will be limited to making choices among the investment options that are offered by the plan sponsor.

Roll Your 401(k) Balance into a New Plan

Another option for treatment of your 401(k) money when you leave a job is to roll over the money into either a traditional IRA or your new employer's 401(k) plan.

Don't try to execute the rollover yourself by withdrawing the money from your 401(k) plan and then depositing it in a different plan. Instead, talk to the trustee of the IRA or new 401(k) plan you want to enter, and explain that you want to roll over funds from an existing 401(k) plan. The trustee will take care of performing the rollover and making sure it is done in such a way that you are not taxed on the money in the year of the rollover.

If you roll your money into a traditional IRA (rolling 401(k) money into a Roth IRA is not an option), you can either roll the money into an existing IRA or set up a new IRA for the purpose of accepting the 401(k) money. It is recommended that you put the 401(k) money into a new, separate IRA instead of mingling the money with money in your existing IRA. That way, if you take a new job and want to roll over the former 401(k) money into a new 401(k) plan, you can do so easily. Only former 401(k) money can be rolled over into another 401(k) plan. If you put the original 401(k) money in an account with money from other sources, you are not allowed to roll that former 401(k) money into a new 401(k) plan.

Your new employer may have a 401(k) plan in which you are entitled to participate. If this is the case, you can tell your new employer that you want to roll over money from an existing 401(k) plan into the new plan. Your employer's plan trustee will take care of executing the rollover.

If you are not immediately eligible to participate in a new 401(k) plan, either leave the money in your original 401(k) plan or roll it over into a separate IRA until you're able to put the money into the new 401(k) plan.

Problems with Rollovers

Although you are entitled to take the 401(k) money yourself and deposit the money into an IRA or another 401(k) plan, there are two potential problems with making the transfer yourself.

First, you must execute the transfer within sixty days from the day the money is withdrawn from your original 401(k) plan. Fail to make the deposit into a new plan within sixty days and the entire amount is subject to income tax and a 10% penalty as well.

Also, if you take the money out of the original 401(k) plan, your employer is required to withhold federal income tax. Twenty percent of the amount in the plan must be withheld as tax. But when you roll over the plan balance into a new IRA or 401(k) plan, you must roll over 100% of the plan amount. Any amount you fail to roll over is subject to the income tax and 10% penalty. So you'll have to come up with the additional 20% that was withheld as tax out of your other funds.

You'll get the tax back the following spring when you file your income tax return, but until then you're out the money.

For example, if there is $25,000 in your 401(k) plan and you want to take the money yourself and roll it over into another tax-deferred plan, your employer will give you a check for $20,000, representing the fund balance of $25,000 less 20% that goes to the IRS as income tax withheld. You can either find $5,000 of your own and make a $25,000 deposit into a new tax-deferred account, and wait to get the $5,000 back as a tax refund next spring, or you can deposit $20,000 into a tax-deferred plan and pay income tax and a 10% penalty on the $5,000 that was withheld.

Partial Payout, Partial Rollover

Another option for handling the money in your 401(k) plan when you leave your job is to take part of the money out of the plan and roll over the balance into an IRA or a new 401(k) plan.

The money you withdraw from your 401(k) plan is taxable in the year in which you withdraw it. The money is also subject to a 10% penalty on your federal income tax return. Your employer will withhold 20% of the withdrawal amount for taxes, and you will be required to pay the rest of the tax money when you file your tax return in the following spring. You may also be required to pay quarterly estimated tax payments during the year to avoid late tax payment penalties.

Because of the steep penalty and the requirement to pay tax all at once on the amount of money you withdraw from a 401(k) plan, it is rarely advantageous to take the money out of the plan prior to retirement. Sometimes, though, you have no choice. If you absolutely have to have cash and there is no other viable alternative, you may have to withdraw all or part of your 401(k) money.

Total Payout

The fourth option for handling the money in your 401(k) plan when you leave your job is to withdraw the entire balance. As mentioned before, this money will be subject to income tax and a 10% early withdrawal penalty on the tax return for the year in which you withdraw the money. You will also be subject to state income taxes under the law for the state in which you live.

The total payout option should be considered only when all other attempts for borrowing money have failed. The cost of money taken out of a 401(k) plan before you retire is exorbitant. Not only do you pay federal and state income tax on the

ROLLING OVER MONEY FROM A FORMER EMPLOYER

If your 401(k) plan contains money that was rolled over from another tax-deferred retirement plan, such as a 401(k) plan from a former employer, your current employer has no hold on this money and you may request a withdrawal of these funds without having to prove hardship to your employer. The money you withdraw will be subject to income tax and early withdrawal penalty.

money at your highest marginal tax rate, but you also pay the 10% penalty. If your federal income tax rate is 27% and your state tax is 5%, that's 33%, plus the 10% penalty, and you're paying 43% for the right to take money that belongs to you.

Hardship Distributions for Employees

As long as you are employed you are not entitled to withdraw money from your 401(k) plan. There are, however, exceptions to this rule. There are four circumstances, referred to as hardship situations, under which you can withdraw money from your plan while you are employed. You are still subject to income tax on the withdrawals and, in most cases, you are also subject to the 10% penalty.

Note that these options are available only if you have exhausted all other sources for borrowing, including a loan against your 401(k) plan (for more information about borrowing from your 401(k) plan, see Chapter 10). If you are eligible to borrow money from your 401(k) plan, you must do this before taking a hardship withdrawal. According to the IRS, you must be able to demonstration an "immediate and heavy financial need" for the money, and there must not be "any other resources reasonably available to you to handle that financial need." When claiming a hardship need, you may have to provide your employer with documentation supporting your efforts to obtain financing elsewhere.

The situations that qualify for hardship distributions include:

1. College tuition. You are entitled to take money out of your plan for college tuition, fees, room and board for yourself, your spouse, and your dependents. The amounts must be due and payable to the school within twelve months from the time you withdraw them from the 401(k) plan. Be prepared to provide documentation supporting the college fees that will be paid with the money you withdraw.

2. Buying a house. You may withdraw money from the plan for purposes of making a down payment on the purchase or rebuilding of a new primary residence. Be prepared to provide a copy of the sales contract for the house you plan to buy. Also provide a copy of a letter from your broker indicating you would not qualify for a mortgage, even if you took out a loan from your 401(k) plan.

3. Medical expenses. You may use money from your 401(k) plan to pay for unreimbursed and uninsured medical expenses for yourself, your spouse, and your dependents. Be prepared to provide copies of past due medical bills as well as an estimate of future medical expenses.

4. Preventing foreclosure. You are also entitled to withdraw money from your 401(k) plan to pay your home mortgage lender if you are facing foreclosure or eviction. Provide your employer with a copy of your foreclosure or eviction notice.

The amount you withdraw under the hardship withdrawal rules is not necessarily subject to the mandatory 20%

federal income tax withholding. Check the guidelines for your plan to determine if this is true. You can request that your employer withhold income tax from your withdrawal, and it's possible your plan allows for you to increase the amount of your hardship withdrawal to cover both the federal and state income taxes that will be applicable.

The amounts you withdraw for hardship purposes usually are subject to the 10% penalty for early withdrawal, and this amount will probably be withdrawn before you receive your money. It is possible, however, to avoid the 10% penalty if you are over age 59½. Be sure to read the guidelines provided by your employer for hardship withdrawals. These guidelines will set out the rules that apply to your particular plan regarding early withdrawals.

Most employers require that employees who take a hardship withdrawal not make any additional contributions to the 401(k) plan for a specified period of time, such as six or twelve months, after the withdrawal occurs.

Starting an Individual (Solo) 401(k)

A new option for the self-employed person is an individual 401(k) plan, also known as a solo 401(k). Other names for this plan are an individual(k) plan or a solo(k) plan. As of January 2002 this option is available for self-employed individuals who want to have an easy option for investing for retirement. If you are leaving the workforce with a 401(k) plan from your former employer, and you intend to begin your own business, consider this new individual 401(k) plan as a vehicle for long-term retirement planning.

You already have the experience of putting aside so much out of each paycheck for retirement. You can continue this habit without missing a beat and not let your new work stand in the way of your long-range planning. Money from your employer's 401(k) plan can be rolled over into an individual 401(k).

Here are the rules and requirements for a solo 401(k) plan:

1. You must be self-employed and have no other employees, although an exception to this rule is that you can employ your spouse and direct descendants and those employees can participate in the plan.

2. Partnerships are also eligible for these plans, but only the partners (and, if applicable, their employee spouses or descendants) are eligible to participate. If the partnership has other employees, the solo 401(k) plan cannot be used.

3. The annual contribution limit for 2004 for a solo 401(k) plan is $13,000 plus 20% of the proprietor's, partner's, spouse's, or descendants' salary, not to exceed a total annual contribution per participant of $40,000. The total amount contributed each year cannot exceed the owner's or employee's salary for the year of contribution. For proprietorships, the total annual contribution cannot exceed the lower of $40,000 or the net earnings from the business, less one half the self-employment tax the business is required to pay. The annual contribution amount of $12,000 will increase by $1,000 each year until it reaches $15,000 in 2006.

4. Plan participants who are fifty or older can contribute an additional $3,000 per year. This catch-up contribution doesn't count toward the $40,000 maximum contribution. The catch-up provision increases by $1,000 each year until it reaches a maximum of $5,000 in 2006.

5. Contributions to solo 401(k) plans are tax-deferred, just as contributions to the employer-sponsored 401(k) plans are tax-deferred.

6. Rollovers are allowed from traditional IRAs, simplified employee pension (SEP) plans, Keogh plans, employer-sponsored 401(k) and 403(b) plans, and government 457 plans.

7. Solo 401(k) plans are also available for C-corporations and S-corporations as long as there aren't any employees who are ineligible for participation in the plan.

8. You may borrow against your solo 401(k) plan, just as you can from an employer-sponsored 401(k).

9. Hardship withdrawals from solo 401(k) plans are available, just as they are from employer-sponsored 401(k) plans. The same rules apply, with the same risk of a 10% penalty for early withdrawal if the plan participant is under age 59-1/2.

10. The plan must be established by December 31 of the year in which you plan to make a tax-deferred contribution. Contributions to the plan for any tax year must be made by the due date of the federal income tax return, including extensions, for the business.

Choosing Investments for Your Solo 401(k)

When you participate in an employer-sponsored 401(k) plan, you are given a choice of how the amount in your

---

SAVING AUTOMATICALLY

If you plan to establish a solo 401(k) plan and want to make contributions during the year, don't wait until the year is nearly over to make your contributions. Set up an automatic deposit plan whereby money is automatically transferred into the solo 401(k) plan from each paycheck or from your bank account once each month. If you wait until the year is over, you'll probably find you haven't squirreled away as much money as you had hoped, or you'll find other things on which to spend the money. Deposit the money regularly and automatically into your solo 401(k) plan and you won't even notice that it's missing.

account can be invested. Typically you are presented with a menu of mutual funds, some riskier than others, and you can either invest your savings in one of the funds or you can split the investment among two or more funds.

When you begin your own solo 401(k) plan, you start from scratch, and you get to choose how to invest your money and who will manage the fund. Begin your research on the Internet, with investment sites like Morningstar (*www.morningstar.com*) or MSN Money (*http://moneycentral. msn.com*). If you don't have Internet access at home, head to the library, where you can not only use computers to study investing on the Internet, but you can also continue your research in the stacks with books about wise investing and saving for retirement.

Most strategists agree that the key to successful 401(k) investing is diversification. Rather than investing all of your money in one type of mutual fund or in one stock (which can backfire, as the 401(k) investors at Enron found out in 2001), split your solo 401(k) investment over an array of funds that provide different levels of risk. By investing in a collection of stocks, bonds, and cash, you temper your investment to the point that you can weather changes in the market. One type of investment may be hurting when the economy is changing, but chances are that all the investments won't tank at once, and at least one of your investment choices will help keep your retirement portfolio intact.

You can set up a solo 401(k) plan with a financial institution or a brokerage house and choose your own investments, but that is only the beginning. Once you've made your investments, you must monitor them over time. Set aside a time at least each quarter to see how your investments are faring and make adjustments where necessary. Determine a plan for how much loss you are willing to suffer in one of your investments types before moving the funds to another type of investment.

For example, if you decide to invest $2,000 in each of three types of funds, and one of the funds dips so that your investment in that fund is worth only $1,500, while the other two funds are growing or remaining stable, you may decide that 25% is the most you're willing to risk in that investment, take your losses, and move the remaining $1,500 to one of the better performing funds. Alternatively, you may decide to weather the investment's downturn and see how it does in the future. How you decide to treat the investments is entirely up to you, but you'll have an easier time deciding when to make changes if you set out rules for yourself before your funds get in trouble.

Another option is to invest your solo 401(k) money into a fund that is already diversified with the mix you want. Many mutual funds include a mix of safe and risky investments, so when one investment does poorly the others can be relied upon to pick up the slack. Examine the actual investment holdings of any fund you are considering as a place to put your solo 401(k) money. Consider whether you would actually want to invest in those individual stocks yourself. If the answer is no, find another fund that more closely matches your choices for investment.

One of the best vehicles for ensuring a comfortable retirement is the 401(k) plan. Don't hesitate to join such a plan but keep in mind this word of warning: Investments are volatile and what seems like a sound investment today may become weak in the future. Monitor your investments closely and don't be afraid to make changes in the way in which your funds are invested.

Chapter 7

Cutting Expenses:
Home Economics 101

WHEN I WAS IN SCHOOL, every student was required to take a class in home economics. In recent years, my own children studied something in school called home economics, but their curriculum was nothing like mine. In their course they learned about nutrition and food groups. Cooking lessons consisted of learning to make powdered drinks and using the microwave to heat up precooked dishes. They learned to sew by making a pillow and stitching a design on top. Practical applications of these basic skills didn't seem to be a priority, or maybe I'm just out of touch with what's practical today. Back in my class, we planned meals, learned how to shop for and store meat and produce, and prepared and served a multicourse dinner to our parents. We sewed actual clothing, we learned how to balance a checkbook, and we learned about the economics of running a household.

Depending on what kind of home economics you studied, the information in this chapter may be new to you or it may be a refresher course. In any case, everyone can use an occasional reminder of how to live economically on a day-to-day basis. This chapter focuses on ways in which you can offset some of the impact of a financial downsizing by lowering expenses. There are plenty of opportunities to trim household expenses without changing your lifestyle.

Cutting Expenses Around the House

There are plenty of ways in which you can trim expenses around the place where you live. Although any one of these tips may save you only a small amount, saving money in a lot of small ways can add up to significant savings overall. Most of these tips are just commonsense methods for cutting your costs.

Cut Your Utility Bill

Look around your house at all the electrical appliances and fixtures you use. How many are turned on that aren't necessary? Make a habit of turning off lights and other electrical devices whenever you leave a room. Here are some easy tips for cutting expenses in the area of utilities, including your electric, gas, oil, and water bills:

- Take quicker showers to use less hot water.
- Turn down the temperature on your water heater; turn it down even lower when traveling away from home.
- Use cold water in your washing machine.
- Turn off the television and radio if you aren't paying attention.
- Water your lawn and garden in the evening or early morning so the sun won't burn off the water quickly.
- Have your furnace cleaned regularly.

- Use more fans and less air conditioning in the hot months; ceiling and attic fans are particularly energy efficient.
- Use fluorescent light bulbs where possible.
- Run the washing machine only when you have a full load of laundry.
- Run the dishwasher only when you have a full load.
- Check your house for drafts and seal the drafts with appropriate forms of insulation.
- Find out if your utility companies participate in a year-round averaging program; it's easier to budget your expenses if your utility cost is the same each month.
- Put a timer on your thermostat to regulate when the house is heated or cooled; this can lower energy costs when you are out of the home or asleep.
- Use timers or motion detectors on outside lights rather than keeping them on all night.
- Don't forget to close your storm windows in the winter, and replace any broken storm windows with new, energy efficient models. Some states (Idaho and Indiana, for example) allow a tax deduction on your income tax return for insulation improvements like this.
- Check telephone bills to make sure all of the long-distance calls are actually yours.
- Check your water, gas, and electric meters to see if they agree with the reading on your bill. In fact, you can test how much power your various appliances use by checking the meter without an appliance running, then checking again while the appliance is running.

Cut Other Household Expenses

There's more to running a household than paying for utilities. Here are two more tips that will help the house run smoothly and economically:

- **Pay bills online.** Take advantage of the Internet for more than looking up recipes and getting e-mail. Use the online services at your bank to pay bills online. You save the cost of envelopes in addition to the ever-increasing cost of postage. You'll also have assurance that the bill is paid on time.

- **Install a security system and a smoke detector.** Not only do you protect your cherished possessions and the people in your house, you can get a lower rate on your homeowner's or renter's insurance.

Cutting Food Expenses

It goes without saying that you can save money associated with your food budget by actually eating everything you purchase and purchasing only what you need. Take a look at how much food you put in the trash as a result of uneaten leftovers or excess amounts purchased. Before tossing bits of food, try thinking creatively about how to use the leftovers in soups and stews and other dishes. There are other ways to save money on food too. Here are some tips.

Clip and Use Coupons

Everybody sees those coupons in the Sunday paper. Fewer people actually clip the coupons. Still fewer people actually use the coupons they clip. And a really small number of people get the best deal for their coupons. The first rule of thumb is to clip coupons only for items you would normally buy. You're not saving money if you get 50 cents off on an item that costs $3.00 when you wouldn't have bought the item anyway but for the coupon. The second rule is, look for coupon sales. Some grocery stores have a policy of doubling the value of your coupon up to a certain amount on particular days, or even every day. Sometimes you can even find a triple-coupon sale and get three times the face value for your coupon. I've had triple-coupon purchases that actually resulted in a refund to me because the item cost less than three times the coupon price. Now that's saving money!

Join a Shopping Club or Warehouse store

The discounts you can get by shopping in bulk at a shopping club can outweigh the annual membership fee. Join with a friend and split the cost of the fee; shop together and you can split the bulk items as well.

Cut Back on Restaurant Meals

Everybody likes to be waited on and to have the opportunity to order new and interesting dishes, especially the person who does the cooking around the house. Recreate the restaurant experience for much less money by having someone else in the house take a turn at the cooking and cleanup duties. Or use the money you would spend on a nice meal out to buy a new cookbook with the types of recipes you would order at your favorite restaurant. Expand your cooking repertoire by trying new things and making the meals at home more interesting. If you can't resist that special restaurant meal, consider ordering the meal for carryout. You avoid the high price of restaurant beverages as well as the gratuity you pay for table service.

Cook According to an Organized Menu Plan

Take the time each week to plan a complete menu for the week, including kids' lunches and snacks. Coordinate your food purchases so that you can take advantage of sale prices, and buy food that can be used for more than one meal. Use leftovers! If your family objects to leftovers, cook less of the main course and supplement your meal with vegetables, salads, and fruits so there won't be leftovers that go unused.

Cutting Transportation Expenses

There are hidden costs associated with providing your own transportation. You may think the cost of getting from here to there is only the cost of the gas you put in the car, but cars cost more than gas. When thinking of car expenses, remember the actual purchase price of the car, maintenance expenses like oil changes, repairs, insurance, and the cost of parking or garaging the car. Here are some tips that can help alleviate some of the expense of driving.

Save Money on Automobile Insurance

There are several ways in which you can cut the cost of your automobile insurance. If you haven't had a moving violation in several years, make sure your agent is aware of this and gives you credit for being a safe driver. If you used to drive to work but stopped making that commute, you can probably reduce the rate of your auto insurance. If you move from a big city to a more rural area, the auto insurance rates are probably lower. If you are insuring teenage drivers in your family, they can get lower rates for getting good grades in school and even for doing well on the driving test. As your teenagers get older and maintain good driving records, their insurance rates will go down. Finally, if you use different insurance companies for auto, home, life, and health, consider consolidating. Insurance companies often give a discount if you buy all your insurance from the same company.

Consolidate Your Errands

You don't have to do the grocery shopping one day, the dry cleaning the next, the post office the next, and the car wash the one after that (in fact, you may want to hire your kids or a neighborhood teenager to wash your car). Keep a list of all the errands you need to run and get it over with in one trip. You'll save time and precious gas money.

Participate in a Car Pool

This is a no-brainer. Whether you're going to work, driving the kids to school or after-school events, or even going to the grocery store, share transportation with others and you slice the cost of doing all the driving yourself.

Talk to Your Employer about Commuting Incentives

Under current law, employers are entitled to create transportation fringe benefit accounts that provide monthly tax exemptions for up to $195 to employees who park in qualified employer provided parking areas or up to $100 for employees who take mass transportation or participate in vanpools to commute to and from work. The money is provided to employees as a salary reduction that is not subject to federal income tax. While the employee is still paying for the transportation-related costs with the salary reduction, the money is received tax-free. There is a movement in Congress to offer a similar incentive to employees who ride bikes to work. Check with your employer to see what, if any, financial benefits are available at your company.

Cutting Clothing Expenses

You need to have clothes, but you may be able to find current fashions for a bargain price. If you sew, you can save money by making your own garments. Here are some tips for keeping the clothes budget to a minimum:

- **Shop resale.** Shopping resale doesn't necessarily mean shopping used. Plenty of resale shops have cropped up in recent years that encourage people to donate or sell new or nearly new clothing items.
- **Sell (or donate) resale.** Follow the same advice given to shoppers and get rid of unwanted clothing items in your closets and drawers. Whether new or used, there's a market for the items you no longer need.
- **Shop off-season.** Buy seasonal clothing at the end of the season when the sales are the best. Also, many of the major stores have closeout shops where they sell the items they've removed from their regular stores at deep discounts. Beware, it's wasteful to purchase clothing for children at the end of the season if they won't wear the clothes until next year—you can't predict what size they'll be next year if they're still growing! If you do buy children's clothing off-season, buy at least a size bigger than what they're wearing this year. If the clothes turn out to be too big, they'll grow into them eventually. If your children have stopped growing, you can make big clothes smaller much more easily than the reverse.

Cutting Debt, Financing, and Other Expenses

We all receive and spend money. We get paid for work that we do, we make purchases, we pay bills, and we borrow.

There are economical ways in which these tasks can be performed. Take a look at these tips and see if there aren't some ways in which you can reduce the amount you spend on managing your money each month.

Get Free Checking

Shop around for a bank with free checking. Some banks give you free checking if you maintain a minimum balance, but charge a hefty fee if you go below the minimum. If your bank has the minimum balance fee, make sure you don't go below the minimum, or switch banks. You don't want to tangle with minimum balance fees because they are too expensive. Let's say you need $500 in your bank account to avoid a monthly $10 fee. By keeping the balance at $500 and avoiding the $10 fee, it's like earning *2% per month* on your $500 savings. Compare this to current savings accounts paying in the neighborhood of 1% per year and you'll get an idea of how much this monthly fee really costs.

Balance Your Checkbook

Many people put off the act of balancing checkbooks for months at a time, and some people don't do it at all. There are several reasons why you should do the bookkeeping every month. First, this is the only way to know for certain how much money is in your account. Sure, you can rely on the amount the bank tells you as the ending balance, but what if there is a mistake? Bank errors are not uncommon, especially if you have a debit card. You can hand your debit card to someone for a purchase, then decide you don't want to make the purchase after all. The amount may have already been charged to your account with no offsetting credit. Don't rely on your bank to keep your account in balance. Another advantage to balancing your account each month is that you have an opportunity to review how you're spending your money. Use your bank statement as a launching pad for making a budget (see Chapter 8 on budgeting basics), and get control over your spending. Finally, knowing what your balance is can keep you from writing bad checks.

Don't Bounce Checks

First, there is the damage to your credit—that alone should be enough. But if you want more, look at how much it costs to bounce a check. Your bank charges you a fee, perhaps $25 or more. If you wrote the check to a store, the store may charge you a fee of $10 or $20 as well. And if the check was for a small amount, say $15, just look at what you paid in fees to have the privilege of writing that $15 check—maybe as much as twice the value of the check. You can ask your bank if it offers overdraft protection, which helps in the short run, but in the long run you're better off balancing your checking account, knowing how much money you have, and spending within your bounds.

Pay Bills on Time

This may seem obvious, but it's easy to let a bill slip past the early payment date. Most monthly bills include a penalty if you don't pay on time. Look at those penalties as an opportunity to save and make sure you don't miss the cutoff date for making your payments. Look into automatic withdrawal from your bank account for your mortgage, rent, or car loan payment. These payments are the same each month and it's easy to set them up so they are paid automatically. Ask your bank about options for automatic payment. There may be a minimal fee for this service, but the fee is much less than the late payment fee associated with those monthly bills.

Stop Using Credit Cards

Keep a credit card for emergency purposes only (unexpected car repairs, replacement appliances) and pay off the balance immediately, the very next month if possible. Don't charge anything else until you've paid off the balance.

Pay More Than the Minimum

Do the math. Let's say you have a $3,000 balance on your credit card and you are assessed 18% interest. If your minimum payment is $50 per month and that's all you pay, after three years you will have paid $180 toward your $3,000 balance and $1,320 in finance charges. At that rate, it will take you nearly thirteen years to pay off your balance, assuming you don't charge another thing to the account. You will have paid $7,750 in interest on your $3,000 charge. If you pay $100 per month on the same account, you'll pay off the balance in a little more than three years, and you'll have paid $1,111 in interest. Make a few bigger payments and you'll tackle that balance in no time.

Use a Debit Card

Debit cards work just like credit cards but charge the amount directly to your bank account. You have the advantage of shopping with plastic and not having to carry a lot of cash with you, but everything you charge is paid for and you are prevented from going into debt for the items you buy. Obviously, you need to keep enough money in your bank account to cover your debit charges.

Increase Your Insurance Deductibles

Analyze your insurance policies, particularly those that have deductibles including homeowner's or renter's insurance, automobile insurance, and health insurance. Reassess how much you have claimed against these policies and determine if your deductible is reasonable. If you don't make many claims, you may save more by increasing the amount of your deductible, paying a lower premium, and paying more for an insurable event when one occurs.

Cutting Entertainment Expenses

You can find ways to entertain yourself and save money at the same time. Won't that make the entertainment just that much more satisfying? Here are some ideas.

Reassess Your Television Viewing

Do you really use all the cable or satellite channels to which you subscribe? If you get ninety channels but find you watch only a handful on a regular basis, you may be able to change your subscription and lower your price.

Go to Bargain Movies

You can watch a movie at 5 P.M. at the local theater for two thirds or less the price of the same movie at 7 P.M. Switch your viewing habits to have dinner after the movie instead of before and take advantage of the lower price.

Most larger cities and towns have second-run theaters that show the newest movies a few weeks after their major theatrical release. If you can be a little patient, you can cut your movie theater expenses even more by catching the show on the second run.

Cut Back on Subscriptions

You can read magazines and newspapers for free at the library. Share a newspaper subscription with your neighbor (and reach an agreement in advance about who gets the coupons!). Buy magazines at used bookstores or library book sales for pennies. Subscribe to magazines in your child's name and take advantage of lower student rates. If you aren't reading a magazine or newspaper that comes to the house, don't renew the subscription. When you're finished with the reading material, pass it along to someone else if you can.

Change Your Entertainment Attitude

Look at the things you do for entertainment and how much they cost. Each time you get ready to spend money for entertainment, whether it's a trip, a movie, the theater, new books, sporting events, or dining out, consider the cost, how much you expect to benefit from the experience, and other types of entertainment that may be less expensive. Instead of travel, look around your part of the country for local points of interest. Consider having your friends from out of town visit you instead of you visiting them. Theaters often put their unsold seats on sale for a reduced rate the day of the performance. You can find books at the library, exchange with friends, or shop the used bookstores. You can watch major sporting events on television, or get a group of friends together and go to a sports bar to watch the event. Look for community fundraisers that offer discount coupons to restaurants. Look for restaurant coupons and specials in the newspaper. Many restaurants have kids-eat-free nights or reduced rates if you order before the dinner-hour rush.

Plan Travel Online

Use Internet travel sites to shop for discount fares on airline tickets, hotel rooms, and car rentals. Few people pay full price anymore with all of the opportunities for discount shopping online. Some popular sites are Expedia (*www.expedia.com*), Hotwire (*www.hotwire.com*), and Orbitz (*www.orbitz.com*).

Cutting Expenses Associated with Pets

The initial cost of acquiring a pet is usually the smallest expense associated with pet ownership. Even if you acquire your pet through a humane society, you will probably have costs associated with neutering and vaccinations. Once the upfront costs are over, the real cost of pet ownership begins. Blankets, toys, food, medical bills, boarding, transportation—it can really add up. Here are some tips for keeping at least some of the pet costs to a minimum.

Search for Vaccination Days

Humane societies and city parks often have free or reduced-cost vaccination programs for pets. Some pet stores, particularly the pet superstores, offer vaccination days as well, with a free or inexpensive vaccination accompanying a purchase at the store. Be sure you talk to your veterinarian before giving your pet a vaccination at one of these places. Your vet knows exactly what your pet's needs are, and your vet needs to know that your pet has been vaccinated so your pet's records can be kept up to date.

Share Vacation Duty

Boarding pets is expensive, so if your pet is sociable consider inviting a friend's pet over to stay while the friend travels. Then you can exchange pet-sitting duties when you travel and save quite a bit of money. Or look for pet-friendly sites when you travel and take your pet(s) along. If your pets are low maintenance, leave your pets at home and have a trusted person in the neighborhood drop by your house every day and care for your pets.

Stay Current with Checkups

Just like people, animals benefit from regular visits to the doctor. In fact, regular annual checkups are even more important with animals, because they can't tell you if something isn't right. Don't skimp on this expense or you may end up with a much greater expense of combating a serious pet illness.

Buy Food in Bulk

Pet superstores offer pet food in bulk. Buy greater quantities and save money on the food. A word of caution: Be sure to store the food properly. If you purchase large bags of dry food, acquire an airtight container for storage so the food won't get stale or go soft in the summer humidity.

Cutting Income Taxes

This last section provides a quick summary of tips for cutting income taxes. These are items that are often overlooked by people preparing their own tax returns. Not all of these tips apply to every taxpayer, but you should find something you can use to reduce that annual bill from Uncle Sam.

Have Your Return Checked by a Professional

If you prepare your own tax return, chances are excellent you are missing opportunities to lower your tax bill. Tax laws are so complicated that the average person just doesn't have the knowledge or the time it takes to understand how to take advantage of all the tax breaks that are available. It's worth it, even if you want to continue preparing your own taxes, to have an expert look over your return and give you some general advice about tax deductions and opportunities that you may be missing.

Check Your Withholding

If you get a big tax refund each year, go over your tax withholding arrangement with your employer or with a financial or tax expert and consider reducing the amount of tax withheld on your paycheck. This money is yours and you shouldn't have to wait a year to collect it.

Review Last Year's Tax Return

In the spring, before you begin preparation of your tax return for last year, get out the prior year's tax return and review it to see what kinds of income you reported and what kinds of deductions you used to reduce that income. For most of us, our tax situation doesn't change much from year to year. Use last year's return as a guide, and gather up all the receipts and forms you will need to prepare this year's tax return. You'll not only remind yourself of items you can deduct and income that needs to be reported, you'll have a nice organized collection of information ready for when you start to prepare your tax return.

Clump Medical Expenses

If you anticipate an increase in medical expenses, such as costs for voluntary cosmetic surgery, or orthodontic work that isn't covered by insurance, nursing or rehabilitative care costs, or other large expenses you plan to pay out-of-pocket, and you qualify for a medical expense deduction on your tax return, try to clump as many medical expenses as possible into one tax year. Many taxpayers don't qualify for the medical expense itemized deduction on their tax return since only medical expenses that exceed 7.5% of your adjusted gross income qualify for this deduction. But if you plan to have enough expenses to get yourself over the 7.5% hump, or if your income has decreased significantly in one year so that the adjusted gross income on your tax return is lower than normal, then take advantage of the opportunity to claim a medical deduction and cram as many medical expenses into one year as possible. Note that you can charge medical expenses at the end of the year and not pay for them until the next year, but still take the deduction in the year the charge was made. If you expect to take a medical deduction, don't forget to keep track of your mileage relating to medical trips. You can deduct 14 cents per mile for the miles you drive for medical purposes (that's as of 2004; check current tax laws for the correct rate before claiming this deduction).

Deduct Automobile Property Taxes

If you pay property tax on your automobile when you purchase it or when you renew your license plates, this amount qualifies as a deductible tax expense on your federal income tax return. You must itemize deductions to take advantage of this tax benefit.

DEDUCTIONS FOR DONATIONS

When donating items to charity for purposes of resale, you are entitled to take a tax deduction for the resale value of the items you donate. However, you must be able to itemize your tax deductions to take advantage of this deduction. (When this book went to press, Congress was considering legislation that would give nonitemizing taxpayers an option to take a deduction for charitable contributions.) If you're not sure how much your items are worth, visit resale shops in your area and price similar items. Online you can use the Salvation Army valuation table at *www.funwithtaxes.com*.

Give to Charity

If finances are tight at your house, you may cut back on your donations to charity. You can still be generous and get a tax deduction to boot if you give noncash items to charity. Clean out the closets and drawers and other storage spaces in your house and you may be amazed at how much there is that you don't need to keep. Don't forget books, magazines, athletic equipment, tools, auto equipment, yard tools, toys, and anything else that is gathering dust. If you don't need these items, stop using your precious space to store them. You may be eligible to take a tax deduction by donating them to a recognized charity, getting a receipt acknowledging your donation, and determining a fair value.

Keep Track of Your Miles

When you drive your car for charitable purposes, such as driving to church to teach Sunday school or help with the pitch-in supper, driving the boy scout troop to its campout, driving the school baseball team to a game (as opposed to just driving to the game yourself so you can watch), delivering meals for a Meals on Wheels program, driving to school to be a teacher's helper, or any similar activity, you are entitled to increase your deduction for charitable expenses by 14 cents per mile for each mile you drive. (Note that 14 cents per mile is the deductible amount for miles driven for charitable purposes as of 2004; the amount is subject to change each year.) Do you believe that isn't worth the trouble? Just try keeping track of the miles you drive for charity in a year and see for yourself. It may be worth your time to track your miles, or it may not be, depending on how much charitable work you do.

Keep Track of Job Search Expenses

If you are looking for a new job, you may qualify for a deduction of certain expenses you incur in a job search, as long as this isn't your first job and as long as you are looking for a job in the same occupation as your last job. In order to qualify for the deduction, there can't have been a substantial break in time since you last worked. Deductible expenses include:

- Resume costs such as typing, printing, and postage
- Other stationery expenses such as paper and envelopes
- Travel costs including car mileage expense at 37.5 cents per mile (as of 2004), as well as air, train, bus and other fares, as long as the expenses are used for trips to interviews
- Fees paid to career counselors and job research facilities such as libraries.
- The cost of meals you eat if you travel overnight for job interviews.

Other expenses relating to your job-search travel, such as taxis, parking, and tips are also deductible. You can also deduct employment agency fees, the cost of publications that list job offerings in your profession, books that contain job-searching tips, and long-distance calls. Job-search expenses are combined on your tax return with other job-related expenses for which you were not reimbursed, as well as union dues, the cost of safe-deposit box rental, and tax preparation and research costs. You must be able to itemize your deductions on Schedule A of your tax return to take advantage of the deduction for job searching. In addition, these are all called miscellaneous expenses, and only the miscellaneous expenses that exceed 2% of your adjusted gross income qualify as an itemized deduction.

Besides all of these suggestions, you can probably think of many more cost-cutting measures that you can employ in your everyday life. Get together with family members or friends and share tips and success stories. The more you share your desire to save with others, the more fun the challenge becomes.

Chapter 8

Budgeting Basics

YOU'VE JUST LEFT your job and on the way out the door you are handed a sizable check representing your unused vacation and some severance pay. This check represents a stipend that can hold you over until you find another job. And it's nice to have all that money, because you feel less strapped. Most people get a carefree feeling when they leave a job, no matter what the circumstances of departure may be. It's natural to harbor fantasies of jetting off to Paris or Hawaii, going on a killer shopping spree, or purchasing the fancy stereo system you've been drooling over for six months

When you wake up from this dream and remember the financial responsibilities which you've committed yourself to, including a lease or a mortgage, car payments, school loans, and so on, you'll probably realize that packing a bag and heading for a South Sea island, a cozy cabin in the woods, or a big dose of Broadway shows may be a fun way to spend your money, but not necessarily the best choice. You can either turn your back on the bills that will inevitably arrive at the first of the month, or you can start a financial plan that will see you through the rough times.

Here are six tips to help put you on a path toward post-employment financial stability.

1. Talk to your family. *You've* lost *your* job and *you* have to make some serious plans and decisions about *your* future—except that it's not just you who is affected here. Your spouse and children and anyone else who depends on you are also affected by the change in your job status. Everyone will have a reaction and everyone will have needs that they want addressed, too. Let your family know about your plan to maintain financial stability, and encourage input and suggestions from family members.

2. Open a new account. Open an interest-bearing account like a money market fund or a bank savings account—something very liquid and not at all risky—and deposit your severance or vacation check in this new account. You can't afford to risk losing your severance or any other money paid out to you upon your departure, so speculative investments like stocks are completely out of the question. Any other assets you decide to liquidate (see Chapter 9) for living expenses while you are between jobs should go into this account as well.

3. Consider new sources of income. If you lost a job and expect to continue working, you need to plan an organized job search. If you left work intentionally and plan to stay home either to raise a family, to begin retirement, to start a personal business, or for whatever reason, you have probably already thought through your options in terms of income that can carry you into the future. If appropriate, make sure your income sources and accounts such as Social Security and retirement funds have been notified that it is time to begin making payouts.

4. Put yourself in a frugal frame of mind. See the tips in Chapter 7 for ideas on cutting costs and saving money.

5. Don't lose sight of the big picture. The urgency of a job loss can make you focus on financial plans for the immediate future—to the exclusion of long-term planning. Keep your eye on goals that are important for you and your family and consider tomorrow's plans in today's budget. You may experience some downsizing today, but that doesn't mean you have to sacrifice the dreams you have for tomorrow.

6. Create a budget. Living on a budget is a good idea any time, but it is an absolute necessity when you are trying to pinch pennies. This chapter shows you how to proceed in creating a budget that works for the present as well as the future.

The Need for a Budget

Most people have a pretty good idea of how much they earn and how much they spend, and if you ask how much people have in their bank accounts, they can usually tell you. But few people really know where they spend all of their money, and fewer still have a method in place that allows them to keep track of the amounts they expect to earn, spend, and save for the long term. No matter what your financial situation is, if you want to get a handle on what is achievable and when you can expect to acquire the things that are important to you, then the information you learn in this chapter may change your life.

A budget provides you with knowledge of your current financial picture, as well as guidance for achieving short- and long-term financial goals so that you can meet life's obligations without dramatically altering your standard of living. When you're experiencing a change in your financial lifestyle, a budget is an absolute requirement for keeping tabs on how much money is available and how that money should be used. A budget also provides you with a playbook for the future, so that when you get a raise, a new job, or an unexpected influx of cash, you know exactly how you can best utilize that money so that you meet your goals.

In this chapter you learn how to create a budget that is flexible enough to meet the changes you encounter in life and durable enough to meet a lifetime of financial goals. A budget is not difficult to make and it's not difficult to follow. In fact, people who use budgets find they can comfortably talk about their finances and their financial goals because they have a thorough knowledge of what they can actually achieve.

Assess Your Goals

You might think that the first step in creating a budget is to get some paper and write down everything you earn and everything you spend. Although you can be sure that's part of the budget-creation process, the first step is to determine your personal financial goals. Don't set financial goals that are completely out of reach, but, at the same time, don't ignore your needs and desires.

If you are single, your goals are your own. If you have a family, be sure to sit down with the entire family and discuss everyone's personal goals. Don't be general; be very precise when you describe the goals, and don't forget to investigate the actual cost of these goals. For example, don't just say that someday you want to provide a college education for your child. Say you want to be able to afford to send your child to the state university, and you'll need to start paying for tuition in 2010, and you estimate you will need to provide $10,000 per semester to cover all the costs.

Be sure to include among your budgeted items an emergency fund that provides a cushion for unexpected events, such as a job layoff, sickness, or repairs (see Chapter 2 for help in developing an emergency fund). Ideally, an emergency fund includes at least three, and as much as six, months of income. If you use some of the money in your emergency fund, be sure to replace the amount as soon as possible.

The financial goals that you put on your list include a lifetime of expectations. Don't just list the items you hope to acquire and achieve in the next five to ten years. You need to think about what you want to achieve for the rest of your life, because there are many long-term goals that can't be reached without long-term plans. For example, if it's important for you to be able to own a house outright without any mortgage by the time you're age fifty-five, you can't wait until you're fifty-four years old to figure out how you can accomplish that goal.

You must consider your long-term goals particularly at a time when you are downsizing. You may be facing some hard economic times right now, but that's even more reason to remain aware of your future goals. Don't lose sight of the direction you want to go in and you will be better able to continue to take steps to achieve your goals.

Remember that the creation of a budget is a family process and that the financial goals of all family members are to be taken seriously. Everyone has different desires and no one deserves to be ridiculed for what he or she feels is important. Everyone in the family has the right to include his or her personal goals in the budget plan, and the initial session is one in which no one holds back. Even if a goal seems unreasonable or unreachable, state the goal and consider its cost. Only when all the goals have been announced and discussed are you ready to move on to the next step.

Categorize Your Goals

Now that you have a wish list of all the things you hope to be able to accomplish financially in your life, it's time to break that big list into smaller lists. Place these headings on four separate pages: "Short-term goals," "Medium-term goals," "Long-term goals," and "Bonus goals."

List each one of the goals from your planning meeting on one of the four pages, in the place where the goal is most likely to fit. As you prioritize, remember that everyone in the family may have different ideas of the importance of each goal. What is a necessity to one person is a luxury to another. Here are some general guidelines to help you determine which types of financial goals might fall into each category, but you have to decide for yourself which goals take priority and when you expect to achieve your goals:

- **Short-term goals** are goals that you expect to meet within one to five years. These goals might include owning a new car, making the down payment on a house, adding a new baby to the family, taking vacations, attending summer camp or private school, taking musical instrument lessons, buying life insurance, and creating a household emergency fund. Many of your short-term goals will seem more like requirements than dreams.
- **Medium-term goals** are goals you expect to meet within ten years. These goals might include purchasing a larger house, making improvements to your current house, traveling, attending college, buying a new car, furniture, or a vacation home, and paying for a wedding.
- **Long-term goals** are the goals you expect to achieve in more than ten years. These goals might include launching your own business, financially aiding your children, retiring, caring for an elderly parent, traveling, and being able to afford future medical expenses and nursing home costs.
- **Bonus goals** are those goals that you want to achieve but can't count on based on your current financial situation.

These are goals that may seem out of reach at this point in your life but that may become reachable goals if, in future years, your financial circumstances change from your current expectations. Goals in this category might include traveling extensively, owning a mobile home, making large charitable donations, and so on.

Calculate the Annual Cost of Each Goal

Now that you've listed all of your financial goals and broken them out by when you expect to achieve those goals, it's time to determine the actual cost for each goal and the years in which you expect to meet that cost. Some goals may be funded in the year in which you plan to meet that goal, other goals may require saving for one or more years.

For example, if you plan to purchase a new car in two years and you want to have a down payment of $3,000 when you make the purchase, you may be able to fund that down payment out of your current savings in year two. If you don't expect to be able to put aside $3,000 for your car in year two, you need to split the down payment between years one and two, and save $1,500 each year, or $125 each month. Write down next to the car how much you need to put aside each year, and also write down how much you expect your monthly payments to be when you purchase the car, and the number of years over which you plan to finance the car.

Creating an Annual Budget

You've determined what your financial goals are and when you expect to meet those goals. Now it's time to analyze your current income and expenditures and create a working budget that enables you to achieve those goals. An annual budget lists all of your anticipated income and cash outlays for a year. At the beginning of each year, create a budget for the year based on the information you compile in this lesson.

Analyze Your Income

List all the areas from which you plan to derive income and how much you expect to receive for the coming year. Your income may be in the form of wages from your job and your spouse's, interest earned on savings, child support payments, rent, inheritance, gifts, and tax refund.

List only the amounts you actually receive. In the case of your job, list the amount you take home on your paycheck, not the gross amount you are paid. If your salary is $40,000, but you only take home $31,000 after taxes and other withholdings, list $31,000 as your income from your job.

For now, don't include other sources of cash such as borrowing, using your emergency fund, or liquidating assets. As you fine-tune your budget you can add the money from these sources later in order to meet your financial goals. Right now, however, find out how much your income will cover, what kind of shortfall exists, and then you can analyze how to meet that shortfall, either by augmenting your revenue or cutting your expenses.

Analyze Your Expenses

List all of the areas where you spend money and how much you expect to spend during the coming year. Include items such as housing expenses, utilities, food, medical expenses, childcare, transportation, clothing, insurance, dues, education, debt repayment, charity, and savings. Include a category for cash allowances and miscellaneous spending.

You may need to spend a month or two carefully tracking how your money is spent. If you like to carry cash and spend money from your wallet instead of tracking your expenses by writing checks or using a debit or credit card, you probably don't have a clear picture of where all your money is spent. Carry a small notebook with you and write down everything you spend your money on. A simple spiral notebook works well for recording your spending activities.

When determining your budgeted expenses, a good rule of thumb is to allow 65% of your take-home pay for regular monthly expenses such as housing, food, utilities, and transportation. Set aside 20% for occasional expenses such as clothing, repairs, books, and fun. Designate 10% for nonmonthly payments such as insurance, and use the remaining 5% (or more, if possible) for savings and investments. Self-employed people need to remember to budget for income tax, Social Security (self-employment) tax, and Medicare tax.

When setting aside money for savings, you need to place some money in liquid investments that you can access readily, and other money in long-term investments that you can leave alone to grow.

Break Down Your Budget by Month

Prepare a separate column for each month of the coming year, then divide each income and expense item by twelve and list the result in each monthly column. You may know of some income and expense items that change or vary from month to month, but for now just enter the same amount in each monthly column. For example, you may pay life insurance once a year, let's say in April. You could put the entire amount of life insurance expense in your budget for April and nothing in any other month. For this exercise, however, put one twelfth of your life insurance expense in each month instead of the entire amount in April.

Total each column to determine how much money you have left each month after all your expenses have been met. If your expenses exceed your revenue, don't worry. You still have some fine-tuning to do to get your budget to a workable state.

Fine-Tune Your Budget

Look over the amounts you budgeted and determine the accuracy of each amount. If some amounts vary from month to month, or if some amounts change during the year, you can adjust the amounts in your budget to reflect the reality of your finances.

Certain amounts that may occur only once or twice a year, such as insurance payments, can be entered in full in the months they occur or can be spread over twelve months in order to help you save for these outlays. For example, if you make a $600 term life insurance payment once a year in July, you can place the entire $600 in your July column. But from a budgeting standpoint, a better approach is to set aside $50 each month to save for this payment. That way the payment becomes just another monthly expense and not a budget buster.

If you expect to receive a raise at your job during the year, or if you expect to start a new job later in the year, enter the change in your income in the month when the raise takes place.

Working Your Goals into Your Budget

Now that you've entered the current income and expense items that you encounter in your everyday life, it's time to work your goals into your budget. Look back at your list of goals and determine how much you need to start setting aside to attain them.

You may discover that you currently don't have enough income to cover all the goals you want to achieve. This isn't unusual. It's easy to wish for things that are currently out of reach. That doesn't mean you won't ever achieve those goals; it just means that you need to take some different steps in your financial planning if you want those things.

Examine your expenses carefully to determine where you can make cuts. For example, if you really want to be able to set aside $200 per month toward your retirement fund, you may need to cut back on your expenses for dining out, transportation, or something else that is less important.

Look back at the cost-cutting measures in Chapter 7 and see how you can incorporate some of those measures into your budget. Also, as a family, consider what other things you can do to reduce expenses. When you are working together to achieve financial goals that you all agree are important, there is much more incentive to cut costs in order to enjoy the lifestyle you want in the long run.

Better still, start thinking about how you can increase your income. It's often easier, and a lot more fun, to earn additional money than it is to cut back on the things you like to purchase. Alternatives include looking for a job that pays more, taking a second job, and trying to improve your skills so you can qualify for promotions or other types of work. If you need more money to meet your financial goals, then it's up to you to figure out how you are either going to make more income or revise your goals so that they are in line with your earning capability.

If you have children of working age, make sure they know what you expect of them in terms of contributions to the family budget. Perhaps they are expected to earn their own gas money or pay for movies and other entertainment. Older children may be expected to contribute to the household budget. Children are more receptive to participation in the family budget if they are aware of how other household expenses are being met. If children know their contributions to certain expenses enable their parents to pay for their college education or a family vacation, they are more likely to want to assume some of the financial responsibility in the family.

College students need to have a clear understanding of what their parents intend to pay for in the way of college expenses, and what they, themselves, are expected to pay for. If students are to receive an allowance, they need to know exactly what their parents expect the allowance to cover. By setting expectations in advance, disagreements and arguments can be avoided later.

When analyzing your budget's performance, keep notes on what goals are currently out of reach based on your current income and expenses. You need to work on developing a plan to incorporate these goals into your budget in future years. Each year you can reassess your budget and adjust the amounts to accommodate the changes in your finances.

Incorporating Other Money into Your Budget

You still haven't adjusted your budget for the use of borrowed money, money from your emergency fund, or money you acquire from liquidating assets. Money from these sources is an important part of your budget.

When you receive money that isn't part of your regular source of income, don't just drop the entire amount into your budget as income in the month you receive the money.

Instead, filter the money out on a monthly basis, showing how much you intend to withdraw from your emergency fund or other accounts as a separate line in the income part of your budget.

If you borrow money, either as a line of credit, an equity loan against your house, money from parents, or money from some other sources, you need to incorporate a payback schedule into the expenses part of your budget. You will also need to factor in the interest you are required to pay on the loan. If you use money from your emergency fund, show the amount you plan to take out of the fund in the income section of your monthly budget, but at the same time think of a plan for putting the money back into the fund.

These payback amounts may not begin in the same month in which you withdraw or borrow the money, but you still need a plan for paying back the money. This payback plan can be added to your medium-range or long-range goals and worked into your budget over time. If you borrow against your house, that loan will affect your mortgage payment immediately so incorporate the additional amount you borrowed.

Budgeting for Taxes

Accounting for taxes is a complicated area of your budget that you shouldn't overlook. Many of the items in your budget will affect your taxes. You should at least have a passing knowledge of taxes so that you can incorporate them into your expenses.

If you record income on your budget at your gross amount of pay, don't forget that taxes will be withheld from that income. If you don't know the exact amount of taxes that will be withheld, reduce your income by an estimate of federal and state income taxes based on the tax rate you paid in the previous year. Also reduce your income by Social Security tax and Medicare tax (7.65% of your gross income), and any other amounts you anticipate having withheld from your pay.

If you have income from interest or dividends paid on investments, or if you sell stocks or shares in mutual funds, there will be tax on those amounts as well. Figure on paying 20% federal income tax on the profit you make selling stocks or shares in mutual funds. Estimate federal income tax on interest and dividends based on your tax rate from last year. Don't forget to estimate state income tax on these items as well, using the rate applicable for your state.

Some of the expenses you include in your budget have an effect on your income taxes as well. If you refinanced your home, the interest on your mortgage payment will change and that amount will affect your tax deductions. If you are paying off college loans or paying college tuition costs you may be eligible for tax deductions or credits for at least some of these amounts.

If you add to your family by having a child, you can take a personal exemption for the child on your tax returns. You may also qualify for an additional exemption if you begin caring for a relative in your home.

Other expenses that may qualify for tax deductions or credits include:

Child-Care Costs

Part of the amount you pay a caregiver or an after-school program to care for a disabled dependent or spouse, or a child who is age thirteen or younger, can qualify for a Child and Dependent Care Credit. The care must be provided at a time when you (and your spouse, if you are married) are working or attending school. The maximum credit allowable in 2004 is $480 per dependent for up to two dependents.

Day Camp Costs

If you pay to send a child under age thirteen to day camp so that you can work or go to school, this expense may also qualify toward the Child and Dependent Care Credit.

Education Costs

Costs of education that are not part of the minimum requirements for your job and that don't qualify you for a new trade or business, can be deducted as a miscellaneous itemized deduction. Included in the deductible amount are tuition, books, lab fees, and transportation to and from the place of education. Miscellaneous itemized deductions are deductible only to the extent that you itemize your deductions and that the amounts exceed 2% of your adjusted gross income.

Job-Hunting Costs

Costs you incur to search for a job are deductible as a miscellaneous itemized deduction, providing the amount exceeds 2% of your adjusted gross income. Such costs include resumes, placement counselor fees, stationery, postage, travel to and from interviews, advertising, as well as research material used in your job search.

Unreimbursed Job Costs

If you spend money on your job and don't get paid back, you can deduct the amounts you spent as a miscellaneous itemized deduction, providing the amount exceeds 2% of your adjusted gross income . Such costs might include, among other things, mileage in your car (other than commuting to and from work), postage, office supplies, long-distance telephone expense, and computer expenses. Be sure to keep the actual receipts to document your job costs. For mileage, keep a diary or calendar showing how many miles you drove, where, and for what purpose.

Medical Costs

You are allowed an itemized deduction for medical expenses you incurred during the year for yourself, your spouse, and your dependents, to the extent that such expenses exceed 7.5% of your adjusted gross income. Deductible medical expenses include doctor and dentist fees, hospital costs, medical insurance, and prescription drugs. See Chapter 5 for a more complete list of deductible medical expenses.

Using Your Budget

Once you complete your budget, don't just file the papers away in a drawer. You need to use your budget and keep it in your mind whenever you engage in financial transactions. If a major change occurs, such as a job change, a move, or the birth of a baby, get out your budget and make revisions.

Keep track of your spending during each month and don't let yourself overspend. For example, if you designate $100 for dining out during the month, keep a running tab to remind yourself of how much you've already spent. If you reach $100 before the end of the month, stop eating out!

Each month, compare your budget to your actual financial activity in order to account for any differences that have occurred. You may find that your first budget does not compare closely with your actual income and expenses. The more you experiment the better you'll become at determining the exact numbers for your budget.

EXTRA CASH?

If you truly have extra money, consider alternatives for dealing with that money wisely. Found cash can give you a boost toward meeting your lifetime goals. You can determine where best to apply the extra money and give yourself a head start toward future planning. Always have a fallback plan for investing extra money, or keep the extra money in your emergency fund to hold for the future in case the next budget detour doesn't go in your favor.

At the end of the year look back over your budget and determine how you did. Did you earn as much as you anticipated? Did you spend all the money you expected to spend? Did you save the amount you intended to? If you come out ahead and discover that you didn't spend as much as you expected or you earned more than you expected, don't just take the extra money and spend it frivolously. The first thing to do is look over your budget and discover what caused the difference. Make sure all of your bills have been paid.

At least once a year, meet with your family and discuss your progress toward meeting your goals. Did you meet all the goals you set for the previous year? Did you have money left over that you applied to future goals? Keeping your family in the loop and allowing everyone to contribute to the family budget decisions prevents untold arguments and disagreements. When all members of your family are aware of how much it costs to operate the household and how much money is available for various expenses, you avoid misunderstandings and enable family members to recognize why certain things have to be accomplished on a particular timetable.

Remember that budgeting is an ongoing activity. Any new monetary event in your life should be incorporated into your budget and adjustments should be made so that you are constantly aware of how much money you have, how much you expect to have, and how that money must be allocated. Year-round budgeting will go a long way toward keeping your expenses under control and allowing you to accommodate unexpected changes in your projected income and expenses.

Chapter 9

Liquidating Assets—If Necessary

ONE OF THE FIRST PLACES people go for extra cash is to their assets. An asset is anything that you own such as a home, a car, material possessions, cash, and investments. A *liquid asset* is something that you own that you can easily turn into cash. In some cases, it makes sense to use your liquid assets to help you through the hard times. In other instances, it can be a mistake to liquidate assets that you've spent years accumulating, and that you need to preserve for your future financial security.

In the best of all situations, you would be able to plan your retirement by strategically and methodically moving your portfolio from higher-risk/higher-yield investments to more conservative alternatives in the years just prior to when you permanently leave the workforce. You would trade speculative stocks for safer bonds, convert risky investment ventures into certificates of deposits (CDs) and annuities, and your tax-deferred retirement accounts would be at their peak, ready for you to begin regular withdrawals for the rest of your projected life expectancy. But perhaps your financial system is not so sound. You may be scrambling to pay this month's electric bill and only half-joking when you say that you'll never be able to retire.

Whether you are the safely invested retiree, the frantic bill payer, or someone in between, the information in this chapter will provide some guidance as to how to access your assets and how to regard your assets at different stages of your life.

Levels of Liquidity

Assets are often categorized into four groups by their levels of liquidity:

- **Most liquid.** These assets are already in the form of cash. This would include money in your checking and savings accounts, as well as any cash you keep in your house or safe-deposit box. You don't have to do anything to liquidate this cash. Depending on your banking arrangement, there may be a fee associated with spending down the balances in those bank accounts.
- **Fairly liquid.** These are assets that have no penalties at all associated with turning the assets into cash, or only small fees for early withdrawal. This group includes money market accounts, certificates of deposit, and U.S. Treasury bills. While there may be a fee associated with turning these assets into cash, the amount is small and doesn't disrupt any long-range growth plans you may have had for these investments.
- **Less liquid.** These assets include investments in stocks, investments in small companies, and investments in real estate. These assets can be difficult to turn to cash on a moment's notice, so ideally you should take this into consideration before you make such investments. How quickly you

can liquidate them will depend on market conditions and the availability of buyers.

- **Least liquid.** These assets include investments in commodities, futures, options, and other derivatives, investments in gold and other precious metals, junk bonds, and initial public offerings. These assets are highly speculative and without a thorough understanding of the market for these assets and complete control over the timing of purchases and sales, you can lose a large amount of money in a very short amount of time.

Risk Factors

When deciding how and when to liquidate assets, you need to consider the risk involved with each type of investment and how the timing of the liquidation affects the value of the asset. There are several factors affecting risk that should be considered if you have any control over which assets you choose to liquidate and in what order.

Market Volatility

The stock market changes on a daily basis. Its performance is influenced by a number of considerations, including economic and psychological factors, supply and demand, and the behavior of investors.

Typically when you purchase stocks your goal is either to wait until the stock increases in value before selling the stock for a profit, or keep the stock as an investment that pays regular income in the form of dividends. Neither one of these scenarios is applicable when you are forced to sell in order to make up a shortfall in current cash. All theories about the longevity of your investment are discarded and you play into the hands of the market's volatility by selling for the best price you can get on the day you decide you need the money.

If you can see that you will be forced to sell stock in the future, monitor your stocks closely to find a reasonable time to sell. If you are convinced your stock will increase in value, you may consider borrowing against your stock until there is a better time to sell.

Inflation

Inflation is defined as the overall general upward price movement of goods and services in an economy, usually as measured by the consumer price index and the producer price index. Inflation has played a significant part in the American economy. You can suffer the effects of inflation when the earnings on your investments fail to keep up with the cost of living.

To see how inflation affects spending, just look at these examples: It costs $100 in 2003 to purchase items that cost $78.92 ten years ago, $54.40 twenty years ago, $24.25 thirty years ago, and only $16.71 forty years ago. Looking at the

HARD LESSONS

Enron employees with all of their retirement investment tied up in Enron stock found their financial future decimated when the company went belly-up. Many other investors, as well, learned too late to follow the sage advice given by Miguel de Cervantes in *Don Quixote*, circa 1605: "'Tis the part of a wise man to keep himself today for tomorrow, and not venture all his eggs in one basket." By focusing your investment solely in one arena, you suffer the fate of that single investment. Investment analysts recommend diversifying investments across several levels of volatility so that you will be more likely to survive crashes, corporate collapses, and other economic disasters.

same inflation calculation in reverse, $100 in 1963 money would purchase $598.37 in 2003, $100 in 1973 dollars would purchase $412.39 worth of merchandise in 2003, $100 of 1983 money would purchase $183.84 in 2003, and $100 from 1993 would purchase $126.71 in 2003.

Changing Liquidity

As your life changes, so must the liquidity of your assets. You are not at the mercy of your investments as long as you monitor and control the way in which your money is invested. Anticipate significant financial changes as they are expected to occur, including the purchase of a new house, college costs, emergency preparedness, and retirement, and adjust your investments by moving money to more liquid investments as your requirements demand. Ideally, at least once a year you should analyze your upcoming financial needs and make plans to move money to a more liquid state if you expect to need to draw on your resources.

Remember that although you can't control the market, you can control where your money is invested, and if you monitor your investments carefully you can be positioned to draw on the most liquid of them when needed.

If you have no investments at all, or have some money tucked away in various investments but not enough to cover all of your anticipated needs, you need to do some fine-tuning to turn your investments into a useful financial planning mechanism for meeting your financial needs.

Begin with an investment plan and diversify your investments to protect yourself from market failures. If your money is placed in one financial institution, check the level of guarantee associated with that institution and make sure your investment is covered should the institution collapse. For example, if you have more than $100,000 in money market accounts at your bank and the bank is FDIC insured up to $100,000, anything you have invested over that $100,000 is at risk. Consider spreading your assets to multiple institutions to reduce the risk of loss from a bank's collapse.

Even in similar investments such as stocks, divide your money across many sectors in order to protect yourself from problems with a particular segment of the market. Mutual funds can be an easy way to diversify your assets because they invest funds in many different sectors of the market.

Life Insurance

If you were to die today, would anyone you care about have to endure a financial loss as a result of your death? If the answer is yes, then you should consider purchasing life insurance. Many people carry life insurance policies, and many others do not, though they know that they should. When considering an investment in life insurance, determine the amount of coverage you should have based on what your family would need in the event of your death.

Young people with no dependents have little need for life insurance other than perhaps a nominal amount to cover funeral expenses. Married people who both work and who have no dependents also have little need for life insurance. Remember, however, that dependents can include elderly relatives as well as children so be sure to plan carefully.

If one member of a married couple doesn't work or makes significantly less than the other, then life insurance on the higher-earning spouse makes sense. Life insurance in this situation provides a replacement paycheck and some financial security to the surviving spouse so that the survivor doesn't have to make a major lifestyle adjustment.

If you have dependents, it is important to consider acquiring life insurance so that your dependents can be cared for and educated should you die. In addition, if you have debts that will pass to someone else when you die, you may want to consider life insurance that will pay off those debts.

The New York State Insurance Department suggests the following needs that you might expect your life insurance to cover:

- Pay off your debts, including medical bills and funeral expenses
- Meet estate taxes and other expenses of settling your estate
- Provide life income for your spouse
- Pay off your mortgage
- Pay for children's education
- Provide funds for retirement for your spouse
- Provide income for your spouse to give your family time to adjust to a new standard of living
- Draw interest to provide funds for some special purpose
- Provide monthly income until the children are grown and out of school

Some of these needs may not be applicable to you, and some may be unnecessary. You can purchase life insurance to cover just medical and funeral expenses, you can use it as replacement income in the event of your death or as an instant college fund for your children, or you can choose to regard life insurance as an investment in your lifetime. Each facet of coverage you add to your life insurance policy increases the cost, and the uses you intend for your life insurance determine, to a certain extent, the type of policy you want.

Type of Life Insurance Policies

There are several different types of life insurance that you should consider, based on your needs and your current position in life.

Term

A term policy has no residual cash value. Term is a pay-as-you-go type of life insurance whereby you purchase the insurance coverage you want and if you don't continue making payments, the policy ends and you are uninsured. The premiums for a term policy are lower when you are young and get higher as you age. Here are some specific features of term policies to keep in mind:

- Some term providers let you lock in a fixed renewable rate with a level premium for a period of several years. This is called level-premium term insurance.
- Some insurance companies offer a convertible term insurance that can be converted to another type of life insurance offered by the same company.
- If you have a renewable term policy and renew it each year, you can usually do so without having to prove you remain in good health. Some term policies require that after a certain age you must meet certain health criteria to continue with the policy.

Cash Value

A cash value policy may be used for retirement income or a child's education, or can simply be held for the life of the insured. There are several types of cash value policies:

- **Whole life.** The original cash value policy, a whole life policy is one you purchase with the intent of keeping it for your entire life. A whole life policy provides a fixed return and a fixed premium for as long as you live. As you age, you can reduce the amount of the premium that you pay and let the earnings of the policy pay part or all of the premiums.

• **Variable life.** This policy also features a fixed premium and a fixed face amount. In this case, however, you control the way in which your premiums are invested and can earn dividend income accordingly. You can borrow against this policy as well.

• **Universal life.** This is also a policy you purchase with lifetime ownership in mind. The amount of premiums and the face value on a universal life policy can vary over the years of the policy. The premiums are invested in a single investment vehicle. You can increase your premiums to increase the value of the policy. You can borrow against the cash value of a universal life policy.

• **Variable universal life.** A union of the variable and universal policies, this type of insurance gives the policy owner control over the amount of premiums paid, the face value, and also the way in which the money is invested.

Redefining Your Nest Egg

As you progress through life, entering different stages of financial necessity, the plans you had for your investments will invariably change. The chapter on budgeting (Chapter 8) discusses methods for changing your family budget to accommodate changing needs. Those changes apply to your design for investments as well as your day-to-day living needs.

Major financial events in your life require a shift of

resources and a change in your plans for those resources. Typical events that cause such a change include the purchase of a house, college expenses, retirement, and the need to tap into your resources for an emergency such as a job loss or a disability. Each one of these events requires a slightly different approach to financial planning and a requirement to either liquefy or at least change the risk level of your investments.

Purchasing a House

When you decide to purchase a house, typically you enter into a bargain with a financial institution whereby you choose a house, you agree to give the financial institution a certain amount of your assets (known as a *down payment*), and the financial institution lends you the rest of the money required to acquire the house (known as a *mortgage*). The mortgage is secured against the value of the house so that, should you fail to make the required monthly payments on the mortgage, the financial institution has the right to take ownership of the house (known as *foreclosure*), and the financial institution may sell the house to pay off the balance on the mortgage.

You may have to liquidate some of your investments to make the down payment on the house. The advantage of buying a house from the standpoint of your investments is that you are really just transferring your money from one asset to another. You switch savings or stock investments for partial equity in a house. Real estate is usually considered a safe investment, assuming you care for and maintain the property. However, you lose the liquidity of your investment when you transfer your money to a house because it's not always easy to sell the house when you need the money, but you usually don't lose the investment itself.

Paying for College

Another type of cash transfer occurs when you pay for a college education for either yourself or your child. If you want to be creative, you can think of this as a transfer of investment—a monetary investment of cash or stocks to an investment in improved earning power and quality of life. That kind of thinking is a bit difficult to quantify, however. If you've planned for college and saved money specifically for that expenditure, you are prepared when the transfer of assets needs to occur.

You know well in advance that you or a family member will attend college, and generally you also know in advance that you are going to purchase a house and thus need a down payment. Because you have advance notice of major life events such as these, you should be able to liquidate assets in an order that suits you, choosing wisely which investments to turn into cash. Here are some considerations when preparing to liquidate assets for college or buying a house:

1. Assets that have appreciated greatly can be liquidated into a lot of cash, but beware the pitfall of too much appreciation being eaten away by high taxes. If you are prepared to sell shares in a mutual fund, look for the shares that were purchased at the highest price and liquidate those first. You'll keep your tax liability to a minimum. (There's more about liquidating mutual fund shares later in this chapter.)

2. Liquidating assets that are tied up in certificates of deposit or other fixed-term investments may produce a penalty if you liquidate them before their term expires. Careful planning can enable you to avoid this pitfall.

3. If you liquidate bonds that haven't reached their full maturity you may receive less than the face value of the bond. Again, with careful planning you can circumvent this problem.

4. Monitor the stock market closely when it comes time to liquidate stocks for the purpose of college or home buying. Try to time the sale of your stock so that you don't take a loss on the investment. When you know you are going to need the money by a certain date, choose a price for which you'll be content to sell the stock, and enter a sell order for your stocks with the desired price. You can enter the sell order yourself if you are trading online, or give the order to your broker who will make the sale for you. If the stock hits that price your order automatically goes into effect and the stock is sold. This keeps you from having to monitor the market every day, hoping for the highest possible price.

5. If you sell real estate to pay for college costs, you again have the situation where careful planning can get you the right price on the property. You know how much you want to get for the property and you know when you'll need money for college. Try to make those two events coincide. If you can't get the money you want out of the property now but you have equity in the property, you may be able to take out a mortgage against the property and use that as a loan for college until the market is right for selling your property.

Liquidating Mutual Fund Shares

When you sell shares in a mutual fund your primary interest is how much money those shares are worth and how much you get to pocket from the sale. There is an underlying issue, and that is how the sale of the shares will be taxed. The tax may not seem significant at the time of the sale; after all, April 15 may be a long way off. However the way in which you sell the shares in your mutual fund can make a significant differ-ence in how your taxes are calculated. It is worth your while to step back, assess the situation, and take the time to make the best sale you can in order to lower your tax bite the following spring.

Different tax rules and rates will apply depending on the amount of time you owned an investment before selling it. Sales of assets are considered to be short-term sales if the assets are owned for one year or less. Sales of assets owned longer than one year fall into the long-term category. There is also an additional long-term category for assets owned more than five years. The computations get particularly tricky with sales of shares in mutual funds because so often the monthly earnings from the funds are reinvested, resulting in additional purchases of fractional shares. This can turn into a book-keeping nightmare if you want to sell only a portion of the shares in your fund.

Average Cost vs. Specific Identification

Whenever you sell shares of a mutual fund, you must report the number of shares you are selling, the date on which you acquired the shares, and the cost of the shares. To ease the burden of accounting for many individual purchases of shares in a mutual fund, the IRS allows taxpayers to

TAX RATES ON SALES OF MUTUAL FUND SHARES

Ordinary income tax rates apply to short-term sales of mutual fund shares. *Ordinary rates* are the normal tax rates you pay on your income earned from jobs or the dividends or interest you earn on your investments. Alternatively, *capital gain tax rates* apply to long-term gains on the sales of assets including shares in mutual funds. As of 2003, if your ordinary income tax rate is no higher than 15%, the tax you pay on long-term capital gains is 5%. If your ordinary income tax rate is higher than 15%, the tax you pay on long-term capital gains is 15%.

average the cost of their mutual fund investments. If you choose to use the average cost method of calculating your purchase price, there are two ways in which this method can be employed. The first method is called the *single category method,* and this method allows you to average the cost of all shares in the fund. Some mutual fund companies even provide shareholders with the average cost of their shares right on the year-end statement.

The second method of averaging, called the *double category method,* allows you to average the shares in two groups. One group includes all the shares purchased a year or more ago and the other group includes all the shares purchased in the past year. With this method, you have one average cost for your long-term sales and another for your short-term sales.

In lieu of using one of the average cost methods of valuing the cost of the shares you sold, you can use what is called the *specific identification method,* which enables you to pinpoint exactly which shares you want to sell. If you use this method you need to tell your broker which shares you are going to sell before the sale takes place. You identify the shares you are selling by specifying the date on which those shares were purchased.

When you use the specific identification method, you can control your profit or loss to a certain extent by choosing shares based on their cost. For example, if you want to lower your tax bite on the sale, choose to sell the shares that cost the most and your profit will be small. Alternatively, if you want a larger profit (one reason for wanting the larger profit may be that you have a capital loss on the sale of some other investment and you want to offset that loss with some gain), choose the shares that cost the least.

In the first year in which you sell shares of your mutual fund, you can experiment with all three methods and choose

DETERMINING THE COST

If you sell all of the shares in your mutual fund at once, the cost is determined by adding up the cost of all of your share purchases, your dividends earned over time, and your capital gains earned over time.

---

the method that is easiest for you or that provides you with the lowest tax. Once you use one of these costing methods to report the sale of shares in a mutual fund, you must continue to use the same method for all subsequent sales from that particular mutual fund. You can use different methods for different mutual funds.

Although it can be a time-consuming process, it's not difficult to calculate your gain or loss on the sales of mutual fund shares. If you take the time to figure out the cost of all the shares in your fund then you'll find that you have a great deal of control regarding how much tax you pay on the profit from your sales.

Taking Money from Your Retirement Plans

Retirement plans including 401(k), 403(b), and traditional IRAs require investors to begin withdrawing money at age 70½ if they haven't done so earlier. You can withdraw money from these plans starting at age 59½ with no penalty. You can also make arrangements to withdraw money from an IRA before age 59½ if you withdraw the money in the form of an annuity and if you continue doing so for at least five years or until you reach age 59½, whichever is longer. The annuity rules are complex and you should consult a tax advisor before making a decision to set up such a plan. If you are eligible to withdraw money from your tax-deferred retirement plans, you'll find there are many specific rules governing how much you must withdraw from your accounts.

Once you begin withdrawing money from a tax-deferred plan, there is a schedule set by the Internal Revenue Service for withdrawing, with regular annual withdrawals based on your life expectancy. The Internal Revenue Service publishes life expectancy tables that are used for determining how much you are supposed to withdraw from your plans.

The IRS Publication 590, Individual Retirement Accounts, provides detailed information about contribution and distribution rules for IRAs as well as the life expectancy tables that are used to compute the minimum amount you are required to withdraw each year. You can download the publication from the IRS Web site at *www.irs.gov*.

Hardship Withdrawals

There are special circumstances under which you can take money from your tax-deferred retirement plans without paying the penalty. These rules govern situations where the plan owner is facing a severe financial crisis, usually associated with unemployment or a medical emergency. The rules are quite strict for withdrawals under the hardship distribution rules, and each type of retirement plan has slightly different rules, but in general you may be able to withdraw money without penalty if you are drawing unemployment compensation, if you become disabled, if you are purchasing a home, or if you are paying college tuition for yourself or your spouse or a dependent child.

Check the rules of your particular retirement plan to see if you qualify for a hardship distribution and, if so, what kind of documentation you must provide and how much you are entitled to withdraw without penalty. Keep in mind that, although you may be entitled to withdraw money from your plan without paying a penalty, you will still owe regular income tax on any tax-deferred amounts that you withdraw.

Liquidating Liabilities

As long as we're talking about liquidating assets, let's take a moment to look at the other side of the spectrum, the liquidation of liabilities. If you have personal debt, which can be in the form of a mortgage, car loan, personal loans, margin accounts, credit card debt, or other amounts you owe, you need to consider the effects of that debt at the same time that you evaluate your assets.

Make a list of all of your debts, showing the amount owed on each, the annual interest rate on each debt, and the number of years of payments remaining. Think about how some of your assets could be used to liquidate your debts and whether or not this is a feasible plan.

Assets earning relatively low interest rates become much more valuable when used to liquidate debt on which you are paying a high interest rate. For example, if you have $2,000 in a savings account earning 1.5% interest, that $2,000 earns $30 a year. Meanwhile, if you owe $2,000 on a credit card on which you are paying 15% interest, that credit may be costing you as much as $300 a year or more, depending on how long you take to pay it off. If you take that $2,000 of savings and pay off your credit card, you still have access to the credit if you need it for an emergency, but your $2,000 effectively earned $300 instead of $30 by saving you the interest you would have paid.

Other debts you own that may be collateralized by tangible items should be analyzed for their worth. If you are in debt for two cars but can get by on one car, sell the second car and pay off the debt. You'll not only save the money you were spending for the loan but you'll cut your costs of registration, gas, insurance, and maintenance on the second car. Prepare a summary to see just how much you spend on that second car during the year. Could you do without the car most of the time, then rent a car occasionally when you need a second car, and still come out ahead?

If you have several years left on your home mortgage, look into refinancing the mortgage at a lower interest rate. The fees associated with refinancing will be well worth it if you can cut your monthly mortgage expense and thus the overall interest you will pay on the loan. Again, I suggest working out on paper how much you can save by refinancing your mortgage at a lower rate. This too is a form of liquidating debt.

Assets are items you acquire as investments, and often they are items you hope will appreciate in value with time. While many assets are acquired with the expectation of eventually selling them, ideally you have control over when they will be sold. When you are faced with a downsizing situation, you may need to liquidate assets before you planned to do so. Give careful thought to which assets you will liquidate and do what you can to get the best price for them. Consider borrowing against assets you want to keep rather than turning everything into cash. One of the reasons you own assets is to help you through the tough times. Even as you liquidate, be glad you have the assets to aid in your time of financial need.

Chapter 10

Borrowing Money

THERE'S NO SHAME in borrowing—particularly when the extra cash helps you get through lean times. The key to successful borrowing lies in developing a payback schedule you can reasonably meet. This chapter explains the ins and outs of borrowing from banks, creditors, retirement plans, and friends and family members. You will learn how interest rates are calculated, the tax effects of borrowing, the importance of your credit rating, and what to do if you can't meet your obligations.

Before you sign your name on the bottom of a loan contract or run your credit card through the scanner, make sure you understand and can afford the amount of the payments you are expected to make, the rate at which the money is lent, and the method used for computing interest on the outstanding balance. You should understand the concept of compound interest and how the interest rate you see on advertised loans is not always the interest rate that you pay. In addition, you need to know if there are penalties for making early or late payments.

There can be benefits to borrowing as well. Some loans

provide a reduction in your income taxes that in effect lower the cost of the loan.

Interest Rates

When you borrow money, there is a fee attached to the loan that is described as *interest*. The rate of interest is presented as a percentage of the amount you borrow and is usually, but not always, expressed in annual terms. For example, a one-year loan of $10,000 with a simple interest rate of 8% would generate an interest payment of $800 at the end of the year. Take that same $10,000 loan, but instead of holding the money for a year, you pay the loan back in six months. The annual interest rate is slashed in half to reflect the six-month time period, so the interest is now only $400.

Interest calculated in the previous examples has not been compounded. The calculation of interest gets a little more complicated when, instead of simple interest, the interest is compounded. The amount of interest you pay can be significantly higher than the quoted rate.

Compounded Interest

When you begin making monthly payments, the compounded interest makes the calculation of payments more complicated, because interest is recalculated each month.

For this example, let's say the same loan of $10,000 is made at a compound interest rate of 10%. In this situation, you pay $879.16 per month, or a total of $10,549.92 over the twelve months. Here's how the payment and the interest are calculated. In the first month, the *principal* (the total amount you borrowed) is multiplied by the interest rate, 10%, resulting in $1,000 interest. The interest is divided by twelve to calculate one month's interest (annual interest divided by twelve months in the year), $1,000 / 12 = $83.33. Reduce the monthly payment by the amount designated as interest, and the remaining amount ($879.16 − $83.33 = $795.83) represents the amount that is applied toward reducing your loan balance.

In the second month, the loan balance has been reduced (from $10,000 − $795.83 paid last month = $9,204.17), so the interest in the second month is calculated based on a lower balance. Interest at 10% of $9,204.17 is $920.42, divided by twelve to determine one month's share, results in $76.70. The loan balance for next month's calculation is reduced by the difference between the payment and the interest ($879.16 − $76.70 = $802.46).

When the loan is fully paid off, you will have paid twelve payments of $879.16, or $10,549.92. Compounding in this manner results in a lesser amount paid on the loan than if you had waited to pay the entire loan at the end of the year. This is because the interest is calculated on a lesser balance each month. Waiting to pay the entire loan at the end of the year puts you in a position where interest was calculated for the entire year, all twelve months.

If you want to borrow money, you can experiment with loan calculators on the Internet to find out how much interest you have to pay and how much your monthly payments will be. There's more information on borrowing online, online resources for estimating payments, and applying for loans online later in this chapter.

Interest on Credit Cards

If compounded interest affords you a financial break as in the previous example, then why do people complain about the high rate of compounded interest on credit cards? Credit card companies are in the business of making money on the money they lend. To do this, they create a minimum payment policy whereby if you pay the minimum payment, your monthly payment covers only the interest and a small amount of principal. Paying only the minimum payments on credit cards extends the life of the loan for years, sometimes indefinitely. Here's an example:

Typically the minimum monthly credit card payment approximates 2% of the loan balance. Say you've extended your credit card balance to $7,000. Your minimum monthly payment is $140. At 18.99% annual interest, your interest for the current month is $110.78. If you pay the minimum payment of $140, you reduce your credit card balance by $140 minus $110.78, or $29.22. Next month your credit card balance is $6,970.78, and your minimum payment, based on 2% of your remaining balance, is $139.42. Interest is $110.31. Paying the minimum reduces your balance by $29.11 to $6,941.67. Assuming you make no more charges on the account and pay the minimum payment of 2% of your balance each month, no more and no less, it would take you eighty-five years to get your credit card balance down to $100 and you would have paid $26,155 in interest on that $7,000 loan.

As you can see, to liquidate a credit card account with compounding interest, you must make more than the required minimum monthly payment. As you make payments each month, the monthly minimum payment amount decreases just a little, so you don't get too far ahead in paying down your balance. In this same situation, if you just paid that original minimum payment of $140 per month, every month, you would pay off the entire balance in 8.3 years. Change your monthly payment to $200 and the balance is gone in 4.3 years. What a difference!

If you have credit card debt, instead of paying the minimum amount and letting the credit card company decide how long it will take you to pay the balance, decide when you want to get that balance down to zero. Then do some calculations to figure out how much you have to pay to accomplish that task and set your own rules for minimum monthly payments. If you have a month or a series of months where your money is too tight to make the higher payment, go ahead and make the minimum payment to keep your account in good stead with the credit card company, then get back to your higher payment as soon as you can afford to do so. And be sure to stop using the credit card for additional purchases—that only adds on more debt!

Additional Costs of Borrowing

Sometimes there are fees associated with borrowing money. Most often these fees appear when you are borrowing a large sum of money over a long period of time. The most common example of a loan that requires fees is a home mortgage. Whether you obtain a mortgage for the first time or refinance your mortgage, you have to pay what mortgage lenders call *points.*

A point is a loan cost that is a percentage of the loan amount. For example, one point on a loan for $100,000 is 1% of the loan, or $1,000. One and one-half points (1.5%) on this loan equals $1,500. One point on a $95,000 loan equals $950. Points are paid up front, in full, at the time that you acquire or refinance your loan.

You may find that points are negotiable and that they are direct results of the amount of interest you agree to pay on a loan. A lender may offer a lower interest rate if you agree to pay an extra point or two up front. If you don't have the money to pay points when you acquire the loan, you face a higher interest rate but a lower up-front cost. When refinancing your home, your lender may be willing to take the points out of the amount you receive from refinancing. In this situation, the lender adds the points on to the total amount you borrow, resulting in a higher mortgage amount. For example, if you agree to borrow $100,000 and the lender adds one point to the loan, you now borrow $101,000.

There are other fees that can be associated with borrowing money, particularly mortgages. Examples of these fees include:

Application and Processing Fees

These fees represent the cost to the lender to process the paperwork on your loan. By assessing application and processing fees, the lender covers its costs should you decide not to follow through on the loan. Some lenders allow you to negotiate to have these fees removed if you actually take the loan.

Credit Report

Before lending you money a lender acquires a copy of your credit report to determine if you are likely to pay back the loan. The cost of this report is generally passed on to the borrower.

Appraisal

Before lending money for a home mortgage, the lender will want some assurance that the home is worth the amount you are borrowing. By making sure that the home has a certain value, the lender is confident that its loan is *collateralized* with the value of the home. That way, if you default on the loan, the lender can sell the home and recoup its losses. The cost of the appraisal is generally passed on to the borrower. Ask your lender if it recommends a particular appraiser. Often banks and other financial institutions have appraisers on staff who perform the appraisal for a fee that is less than you might pay if you sought out your own appraiser.

Early and Late Payments

Before you agree to borrow money, find out if there are penalties assessed if you make payments ahead of schedule. You may not have the wherewithal to make extra payments at this point in your life, but later on, if your financial situation improves, you might like to put an end to the loan payments and pay off the balance. Or, you might borrow at one interest rate today and have an opportunity to pay off the loan by borrowing at a lesser rate in the future.

Also find out how additional interest is assessed or what type of fee might apply if you make a late loan payment. The potential for such additional fees should be considered when assessing the cost of borrowing money.

If your financial downsizing contemplates long-term planning, as it should, and if there is no penalty for making early payments on your loans, consider the savings involved in making early payments. A thirty-year mortgage for $80,000 at 8% results in 360 payments of $587.01 over the thirty-year period, or $211,323.60. Make thirteen instead of twelve payments per year, and you can reduce the period of the loan to twenty-three years and a total of 299 payments for approximately $162,000. Look at all the money you save by just making one extra payment per year on the loan! When you make an early payment, the entire payment goes to principal, thus reducing the amount on which interest is calculated in the future months.

Tax Benefits of Borrowing

The interest on certain types of loan payments can generate tax deductions on your income tax returns. These tax deductions can be factored into your calculations for how much money you can afford to borrow because in effect the tax savings reduces the amount of money you pay for a loan and increases the amount of money at your disposal. Many years ago, nearly every type of interest you paid produced a tax deduction, but more recently, the Internal Revenue Service has become more restrictive regarding what types of loan interest may be deductible. For our purposes here, interest payments that are tax-deductible include interest on a mortgage, interest on money borrowed from investments, and interest on money borrowed for business purposes.

Interest Paid on Your Home Mortgage

The interest on the mortgage loans at your principal place of residence produces a tax deduction. In the year in which you first receive the mortgage loan, you may pay points, sometimes called loan origination fees, as an up-front cost of borrowing the money. This cost is tax deductible as well. The interest paid on a second mortgage on your principal residence is also tax deductible. You must itemize your tax deductions in order to take advantage of these deductions.

Mortgage interest on a second home is tax deductible, but a deduction for mortgage interest on any other residence you own for personal purposes is not allowed as a tax deduction.

Home equity interest (interest on a loan secured by the value of your home) is also deductible to the extent that the loan does not exceed the fair value of your home less any other outstanding loans.

The points you pay for the mortgage on a second home, as well as any points you pay for a second mortgage on a primary home, cannot be deducted in full in the year that they are paid. Instead, these points are amortized (spread out) over the life of the loan. A fifteen-year mortgage on a second home for which you pay $1,500 in points generates a tax deduction of $100 for each of fifteen years. Should you sell the home before the points have been fully amortized, you are allowed to take a tax deduction for the remaining unamortized amount in the year of the sale.

Investment Interest

Interest you pay on money borrowed for investment purposes, such as interest on a margin account at a stockbroker's firm, can be deductible on your tax return with certain restrictions. Typically, profit earned on investments is subject to tax at a favorable rate, lower than the regular income tax. If you choose to take a deduction for the interest you pay in order to maintain these investments, the investment profit on which you can use favorable tax rates is reduced by the amount of interest you choose to deduct.

Deducting the investment-related interest is optional and you should calculate your income tax with and without the interest deduction to see which method gives you the greater tax savings. You must be able to itemize your deductions in order to take the tax benefit of a deduction for investment interest that you paid.

Business Interest

If you own rental property or other business property for which you have borrowed money, the interest you pay on the amount you borrow is deductible as a business expense.

If you use your vehicle for business, the *business portion* of the interest on your car loan may be deductible as a business expense. The business portion is calculated by dividing the number of miles you drive your car in a year for business by the total number of miles you drive in the year for all purposes, which produces a business percentage.

If you are an employee and you use your vehicle for business purposes, the deduction for vehicle interest is available only if you itemize your deductions. If you are self-employed, you can take the deduction for the business portion of your vehicle interest on your business tax form (typically Schedule C).

Personal Interest Is Not Deductible

Interest on amounts borrowed for personal purposes, such as interest on credit card debt or interest on a vehicle loan when the vehicle is used strictly for personal purposes, is not allowed as a deduction on your income tax return. There was a time when a deduction for this type of interest was allowed, but there is no provision for such a deduction today.

Borrowing from Your 401(k)

If you are a participant in a 401(k) or similar tax-deferred retirement plan, you may have an opportunity to make a loan to yourself from the vested amount in your plan. Some 401(k) plans do not allow for loans—it's up to employers to decide if company plans have this feature or not—so check with your employer or 401(k) plan administrator before counting on the ability to borrow from your plan.

If you do have the right to borrow from your 401(k) plan, you may be restricted on how the borrowed funds can be used. Some plans allow borrowing only for educational purposes, medical expenses, purchasing a home, or to prevent eviction from a home. Other plans that allow borrowing may have no such restrictions. Your 401(k) plan documentation will describe what, if any, loan availability comes with your plan.

Borrowing from a 401(k) plan can be an easy place to turn to for a low-interest loan. You don't need to plead your case to an unsympathetic loan officer; the money is yours and you are entitled to take it. And when you pay the loan back, the interest that accompanies your payments goes into your plan. Not a bad deal for a loan arrangement! There are some red flags, however, that you need to watch out for when you borrow from your tax-deferred plan, such as limits on how much you can borrow and the frequency with which you can borrow. You may be prevented from making additional contributions to your plan for a period of time after you take out your loan. Also, you need to consider the implications of your loan should you leave your job before the loan is paid off.

How Much Can You Borrow?

The most you can borrow from your 401(k) plan is the lesser of $50,000 or 50% of the vested balance in the plan. To be vested, the money must belong to you. If your employer makes contributions to your plan, the money may not be immediately vested, so your access to your employer's share of plan contributions may be limited or entirely unavailable. The amounts that the employer contributes usually become vested based on the number of years you spend with the company. You'll have to read your plan documentation or check with your employer to find out how vesting works with your plan. You can also contact your plan administrator to find out how much of your plan balance is available for you to borrow.

You may be limited in the frequency with which you can borrow from your 401(k) plan. Some plans prevent you from taking more than one 401(k) loan at a time. Others allow you to borrow as often as you want from your plan, as long as there are funds available to borrow. If you already have a loan outstanding, an additional loan will be based on the remaining vested balance in the plan, which may be quite a small amount if you've already borrowed the maximum.

Advantages to a 401(k) Loan

In addition to a reasonable interest rate and a complication-free loan process, there are other advantages to borrowing from a 401(k) plan. If you are determined to tap into the money residing in your 401(k) plan, you can take out a loan and avoid the taxes normally present on a 401(k) withdrawal.

The loan proceeds are not subject to income tax, and there is no nasty 10% penalty for withdrawing money from the plan in the form of a loan. That, of course, assumes you intend to pay the money back on a timely basis and follow through with those intentions.

Paying Back Your 401(k) Loan

Payback of your 401(k) loan begins immediately after you take the money. You determine the payback period, up to a maximum of five years, unless you are using the money to purchase a house. If the money is for a house, you may have a longer period of time to pay back the loan, depending on the terms of your company's plan.

Your employer will withhold loan payments from your paycheck and make the payments in the same way that 401(k) contributions are withheld and paid to the plan administrator. Because your employer is involved in the payback process, you must understand that there is no privacy between you and your employer about your borrowing money.

Payback Requirements If You Leave Your Job

You should keep one thing in mind if you borrow money from your 401(k) plan and subsequently quit or lose your job before the loan is paid back. Depending on the terms of your 401(k) arrangement with your employer, you may be required to pay back the entire loan balance when you leave your job.

By all means, before borrowing money, find out the payback requirements in the event of a job cessation, and be prepared to pay back the entire loan, if necessary, at the time your employment ends.

If you are required to pay back your loan all at once and can't do so, the plan administrator will pay back the loan from the remaining balance in your plan (that way your loan is always protected since you can never borrow more than one half the balance in your plan). If this happens, the payback amount is treated like a withdrawal from your plan and you will have to pay income tax and penalty on the withdrawal.

Borrowing for College

Most colleges participate in financial aid programs that provide financial assistance to students and their parents. A standard form, the Free Application for Federal Student Aid (FAFSA), is required by most schools if students are applying for aid. In a way, an advantage to downsizing your income is that you qualify for more financial aid according to the FAFSA formula. You can fill out the FAFSA form either on paper or online at *www.fafsa.ed.gov* and you will be told exactly how much financial aid your family qualifies for.

When you apply for college for yourself or your children, the college looks at the FAFSA form when determining how much financial aid to offer. Many colleges now are "need blind," meaning they make their acceptance decisions without looking at a family's ability to pay for the education, and then they offer a package of loans, grants, and work study based on the family's FAFSA results. If you experience a sudden downsizing but have set aside money for college based on a higher income, you may not qualify for increased financing since you are required to report your savings as well as your income on the form.

Borrowing Online

If you own a computer and have access to the Internet you have the ability to shop for loans online and experiment with different loan scenarios. Not only can you actually apply for a loan and get loan approval from the comfort of your desktop computer, but you can use loan calculators to determine how much a loan really costs and you can compare the cost of various loans without ever having to leave your desk.

If you plan to rely on the Internet to acquire a loan, make sure you know exactly what loan terms are available and what loan terms you want, and make sure you can find exactly those terms from a lender you feel is reliable. Alternatively, you can use the Internet to explore borrowing options, then take that information with you when you meet with a loan officer at your financial institution. You can't negotiate a loan online; you can take only the terms that are offered. However, when you meet with a lender in person you may be able to negotiate a lower rate or a release from penalty for early payment. You can also get all of your questions answered if you meet with a loan officer in person.

Online Loan Calculators

Online loan calculators tell you how much your payments are on a loan of a particular amount. In addition, a loan calculator tells you how much you can afford to borrow, thus giving you an idea of how much a lender will be willing to lend you. For example, if you are interested in purchasing a home that costs $125,000, a loan calculator asks you to enter information about your annual income and your current debt. Using this information, the calculator might tell you that a typical bank lends $80,000 to someone in your income/debt bracket. Now you know that either you can't afford to purchase the house or you need to find a way to come up with a down payment of $45,000. Using the loan calculators listed at the Web sites later in this chapter, you can also consider costs of refinancing existing debt and debt consolidation loans. You can also use the calculators to figure out how much you should pay in monthly payments if you are borrowing from a friend or family member.

Shopping for a Mortgage

When you shop for a mortgage online, you find out the range of interest rates that lenders currently are offering, the standard number of points that accompany those interest rates, and the amount of monthly payment you can expect to make. By filling out a mortgage calculator, you also learn the type of information about your personal finances that a mortgage lender expects you to provide.

Sometimes mortgage lenders agree to a lower down payment on a homeowner's loan if you agree to pay *private mortgage insurance* along with your monthly payment. The private mortgage insurance increases your monthly payment for several years. Typically, when the equity (the appraised value of the house less the amount collateralized by your mortgage) in your house exceeds 20%, you can stop paying the private mortgage insurance.

Shopping for an Auto Loan

Shopping for automobile loans is also easy to do on the Internet. Many automobile manufacturers have their own loan program, and financial institutions also lend money for automobiles. By exploring various options on the Internet, you know what terms are available before you begin the process of negotiating in person for a loan. Rather than being surprised at the bank, you can find out the rate of interest other lenders are offering and determine how much your monthly payment will be.

Your Credit Rating

From a financial point of view, your credit is your pedigree. An excellent credit rating means stores and banks trust you to carry their credit cards and charge your purchases, and they are confidant that you can make your payments regularly and on time. When your personal finances are in dire straits, your credit rating is at risk. And, unfortunately, this is the riskiest time to treat your credit rating carelessly. When you're in financial distress, you may need access to borrowing power. Endangering your credit rating endangers your ability to borrow, and failed attempts to borrow exert further damage on your credit. It's a vicious circle.

Flaws in your credit history mean that you might pay more interest on the purchases you charge, or you might not be able to get a credit card or extend the credit limit on a card you already own. Lenders are happy to provide loans to people who have a good credit history; they are less likely to accommodate those who look like a risk. Some employers even check credit histories of job candidates, so a bad credit history can affect your ability to get employment.

You can establish good credit, you can control your credit rating so that it remains positive, and you can repair a bad credit rating. To do so, you need to know what creditors look at when they judge your credit, how you can check your own credit rating, and what you can do to improve an unsatisfactory rating.

How Credit Is Established and Judged

When you first become a consumer, you start with a clean slate. There is no recorded history of how you spent your childhood allowances and amounts you earned from odd jobs, or how well you budgeted your money so that you would have enough cash at the end of the year to buy holiday presents.

As soon as you open a checking account or get your first credit card, all that changes. Now the watchful eyes of the credit companies are upon you and your financial transactions become a roadmap to your purchasing and spending habits. From this point forward there is a recorded history of your credit transactions and any transgressions, such as overdue payments, that relate to your spending experiences.

When you apply for a credit card, even if you don't accept the card, a credit report is made. If you make a late payment on a credit card, a credit report is made. If you overdraw your checking account at the bank, a credit report is made. These reports are created by the company that issues the credit card or by the bank where you have your account and are sent to the companies that keep track of credit activities.

There are three companies that track the credit activities of American consumers: Equifax, Experian, and TransUnion. These companies maintain records on anyone with a recorded credit history, and make their reports available to any company or organization that wants to check on the history of an individual.

Information That Appears on a Credit Report

Several types of information appear on your credit report. You'll find the name of all the companies to which you owe money and the amounts that you owe. You'll see the length of time each account has been open. The report also lists your relationship to credit transactions. For example, if you are married and a debt is jointly owned by you and your spouse that information appears on your credit report.

The credit report also shows any history of late payments on each account that is tracked, and the current status of the account. An account might have been paid in full so the current status is that the account is closed, but the history of the account may still appear on the report. In addition, the credit report includes public records of liens, repossessions, foreclosures, and bankruptcies in which you have been involved. Typically, information about your payment history stays on your credit report for seven years.

When you apply for a credit card, the store or financial institution that issues the card requests a copy of your credit report from one of the three companies mentioned earlier. A decision is made about whether or not to issue the card and how much credit to give you based on the information in the credit report.

Request Your Own Credit Report

You can purchase your own credit report from Experian, TransUnion, or Equifax, the credit report companies mentioned earlier. The price is low; it ranges from $8 to $25 dollars per report. However, should you be rejected for credit based on a report from one of these credit report companies, the business that rejected your credit must tell you which company supplied the report on which the decision was based, and the credit report company can provide you with a copy of your credit report for free.

You can contact the credit report companies by telephone, by mail, or right on the Internet. Costs of credit reports vary depending on the state in which you live and other circumstances, such as whether or not you have recently been rejected for credit or whether or not you have recently applied for a credit report.

Experian
1-888-397-3742
www.experian.com/consumer

TransUnion LLC
Consumer Disclosure Center
P.O. Box 1000
Chester, PA 19022
1-800-888-4213
www.transunion.com

Equifax Credit Information Services, Inc.
P.O. Box 740241
Atlanta, GA 30374
1-800-685-1111
www.Equifax.com

You can also request credit reports from all three credit report companies at once through these Internet sites: *www. credit411.com, www.lendingtree.com,* or *www.banksite.com.*

Common Credit Report Errors

Don't assume the information on a credit report is correct just because the information has been published. Credit reports are not infallible. In fact, a study performed by the Consumer's Union found that nearly half of the credit reports in circulation contain errors or outdated information. It's wise to obtain a copy of your credit report from time to time and examine the report for accuracy.

Common errors that appear on credit reports include outdated information such as account balances that have been paid off but not cleared from the report, credit claims that were resolved in your favor but that still appear on the report, and financial information of a former spouse, or information of another person who has been confused with you.

Take Control of Your Credit History

You can take steps to correct any erroneous information that appears on your credit report. Here's what you should do:

1. Notify the credit bureau. Contact the company that prepared the erroneous report and provide evidence of the error. If an account has been paid off or a dispute has been resolved, send copies of the statement on which the payment was recorded or the paperwork that reflects the resolution of the dispute. If the wrong person's information appears on your report, let the company know of the mistake and confirm your name and Social Security number with the credit bureau.

2. Ask for a correction form. Companies that issue credit reports have official forms you can use to describe the problem that appears on the report and provide a resolution to that problem.

3. Notify the creditor. When erroneous information appears on your credit report, it may be a result of incorrect information provided to the credit bureau by your creditor. Ask your creditor to submit an updated credit notification to the credit bureau on your behalf.

4. Check with other credit bureaus. Remember there are three companies that issue credit reports. Bad information on one credit report may appear on the reports of the other companies as well. It's wise to get a copy of all three reports and clean up problems on all reports at one time.

5. Request another copy of the credit report in ninety days. Give the credit bureau three months to straighten out the problem, then request a new report to make sure that all the information is now correct.

6. Remember there is a seven-year statute. The credit bureau is obligated to remove information about closed accounts from your report once seven years has passed. If you had a bad experience in your past and failed to make timely payments to a creditor, but eventually cleared the account, the history of that account must be removed from your credit report seven years after the account was cleared. If there is out-dated information on your credit report you can ask and expect the credit bureau to remove the information.

7. Add a personal comment. If you disagree with some information that appears on your credit report or want to add an explanation, you have the right to place a 100-word statement on your report. For example, perhaps you are divorced and some debts that appear on your credit report were incurred while you were married but actually belong to your ex-spouse. The credit bureau may not agree to remove the debts from your credit report, but you can provide an explanation of your marital status and the ownership of the debts that anyone who reads the report can see.

It's a good idea to request a copy of your credit report before you borrow money. For example, if you want to purchase a house and are planning to apply for a mortgage, get your credit report and make sure everything on the report is accurate. Correct any problems that exist so that your credit report portrays you as an excellent credit risk.

Make Yourself a Good Credit Risk

Consider the following steps as ways to create a credit history that makes you look like a good credit risk.

Sign Up for a New Credit Card

When you apply for a credit card, the fact that you made such an application appears on your credit report. Use the card and make payments of at least the minimum amount due each month and on time. This practice demonstrates that you can manage your credit card and budget your expenses. If possible, don't just make the minimum payment each month but pay off the credit card balance quickly. A prompt payoff of credit can improve your credit history.

JUST A FEW CARDS

Don't sign up for lots of credit cards. There's such a thing as too many credit cards. Sign up for a multitude of credit cards and it might look like can't manage your finances with a reasonable amount of credit.

Be careful when signing up for credit cards if your credit is already at risk. Each time you apply for a credit card, a notation is made on your credit report. It is also noted whether or not you were awarded the card, so if you receive rejections for credit card applications, those rejections will appear on your report for other potential lenders or credit card companies to see.

Borrow Money and Make Payments on Time

When you borrow money for a home or car, or make any consumer loan, be sure to make your monthly payments on time. Timely payments make you appear to be a good credit risk. Overdue loan payments make you look like a bad credit risk. Late mortgage payments and car payments are particularly dangerous to your credit.

Have Someone Cosign a Loan with You

If you are unable to borrow money on your own or are just getting started establishing your credit, ask a parent or someone else who agrees to take the risk with you to act as a cosigner on a loan with you, then make all the payments yourself and on time. This process helps establish your credit-worthiness so the next time you might be able to borrow the money on your own.

Get a Secured Credit Card

A secured credit card is like a credit card with a savings account attached. You place a certain amount of money in an account, then you get a credit card that you can use up to the balance of the account. For example, you might place $1,000 in a secured credit card account. Typically this is an interest-bearing account. You receive a credit card that has a $1,000 line of credit. You can use the card at any place where credit cards are accepted, but you can charge only up to $1,000 total on the card. If you're coming out of a bad credit situation, this is a safe and excellent way to begin rebuilding your credit. Secured credit cards are also good credit alternatives for people who have trouble keeping a limit on their spending. With a secured credit card you cannot exceed the limit of the balance in the account; you can spend only as much as you deposit in advance.

A secured credit card is indistinguishable from a regular credit card. When you use the card, a vendor can't tell that the card is secured. The money you use to secure the card is yours, and you have the right to close the credit card account and recover any remaining balance in the account.

Here are some companies that provide secured credit cards:

Wells Fargo
1-800-642-4720
www.wellsfargo.com

Washington Mutual
1-800-649-4090
www.wamu.com

Get Help with Credit Problems

If you can't make the payments to which you committed, such as credit card payments, monthly utilities payments, mortgage, taxes, and so on, don't go into hiding, hoping the creditors won't notice. It's your attempts to avoid bills, letters, and phone calls that will get their attention. Keeping the lines of communication open is your best chance of getting reasonable treatment from your creditors.

If you have difficulty with credit, you can seek help from a consumer advocate or debt counselor. These people assist with credit problems and help consumers develop a plan to pay off bills and build a good credit history. You can find out more about consumer advocates on the Internet at *www.credit infocenter.com.*

You can also perform an Internet search or look in your telephone book for a Consumer Credit Counseling Service in your state. These services help you organize and find means to pay your debts. They can help negotiate lower payments and even reductions in the amounts you owe, and they act as an intermediary between you and your creditors, helping to keep your creditors at bay while you go about the business of making your payments. Consumer Credit Counseling Services can help you with budgeting as well as running interference with the companies to whom you owe money.

Where to Begin When Your Debts Are Too High

As soon as you realize you are facing a financial squeeze and won't be able to pay the bills you owe, get busy and revise your budget based on your current stream of cash. (See Chapter 8 for more information about working with budgets.) Updating your budget to reflect your current earning and spending will give you a starting point for speaking with your creditors realistically about your ability to pay your debts. By analyzing your budget you'll be able to see where your money is going and where, if possible, you can cut back to make more money available for your creditors.

Once you know exactly how much money you have available for your debts, make a list of all of the amounts you owe and prioritize the list in order of which payments are mandatory, such as mortgage or rent, taxes, and utilities, which ones are amounts you are unlikely to be able to bargain with, such as childcare, automobile payments, or insurance, and which ones you think you may be able to consolidate and perhaps reduce, such as credit card payments. Also list the items that are very flexible, such as gifts, entertainment, and dining out.

Examine your spending, particularly the flexible items, and search for ways that you can reduce your monthly expenses and thus increase the amount of money you have to pay your creditors. Chapter 7 provides suggestions for cutting back on common expenses.

Next you need to start making calls. Either call individual creditors yourself or meet with a debt coordinator whose business includes making such calls. Explain your current shortfall succinctly and matter-of-factly without dwelling on your plight but instead focusing on your desire to accommodate creditors while getting yourself back on your financial feet. You'll be pleasantly surprised at how many lenders, particularly those in the credit card group, and even those in the mortgage and utilities group, are willing to work with you to reach some payment terms that are feasible.

If you don't get anywhere negotiating on your own, by all means get a professional debt counselor to intervene on your behalf and make payment arrangements for you. It is possible to consolidate and reduce payments. If you expect your financial situation to improve in the future, you may also be able to negotiate a cutback in current payments with the understanding that you will make up the shortfall after a certain amount of time has passed.

Useful Web Sites for Information on Borrowing

You can find loan calculators, information about borrowing, including current rates of interest on various types of loans, and links to online lenders at these sites:

MortgageExpo.com
www.mortgageexpo.com

Bankrate.com
www.bankrate.com

Mortgage.Interest.com
www.interest.com

RateNet
www.rate.net

Fannie Mae Foundation/Home Buying Guides
www.fanniemaefoundation.org/programs/hbg.shtml

BankSite
www.banksite.com

Credit Info Center
www.creditinfocenter.com

Remind yourself that there is no shame in borrowing. Borrowing is a useful tool. Successful borrowing can help you through lean times. Borrow what you can afford to pay back, and seek help instantly if it appears you are getting in over your head.

Chapter 11

Taking Temporary Work

ONE OF THE OPTIONS you can consider when changing your financial lifestyle is taking temporary work. Temporary work can be either full-time or part-time. With temporary work, you might have a hope, or even an expectation, that the temporary assignment will lead to something more permanent, but the initial commitment to the job is that of a temporary worker.

One reason you might have for exploring the temporary workforce is a desire to work in an environment where there is less expectation of employee longevity. For example, if a spouse anticipates a transfer in the near future, or if you are returning to the workforce after starting a family, you may be more comfortable working for an employer who doesn't expect you to commit to a long-term position. You may be between jobs and in need of a paycheck, or you may be expecting to take a permanent job that won't be available for a certain period of time.

Whatever your reason for taking a temporary job, this type of work demands a different frame of mind from that which you might have on a permanent job. You're trading flexibility and lack of commitment for a paycheck, but don't expect to necessarily be treated as you would be if you were a new full-time employee. Your opportunities for advancement and training may be limited, your options on choice office space or best selection of work assignments may be the least attractive, and you rarely qualify for benefits.

The Pros and Cons of Temporary Work

Temporary work is nonpermanent work that sticks closely to the employee objective of earning money and the employer objective of getting a job done. The concept of temporary work strips away the deeper meaning of career and commitment and focuses on the essential needs of employer and employee.

Employers like temporary workers because the company doesn't have to pay benefits, nor does it have to pay much for training—typically, temporary employees are already trained for the job. Also, if the temporary employee doesn't work out, there's little risk on the employer's part; the employer can declare an end to the temporary assignment and be done with the employee.

Employees like temporary work because it offers flexible hours, the opportunity to learn new skills, exposure to new business opportunities, and the potential for being hired full-time. And, if they don't like the working environment, they can leave, guilt free.

Temporary work is on the rise. According to the U.S. Bureau of Labor Statistics, the number of temporary workers in the United States has increased from fewer than 600,000 in the 1980s to 2.5 million in 2000. The number of temporary workers is expected to increase by more than one million additional workers by 2006. One reason cited for the increase in temporary work is the change in the climate of U.S. businesses. No longer can a dedicated employee expect a lifetime of security from a single employer. Ruthless layoffs resulting from mergers, downsizing, and corporate failures have lowered expectations of workers and employers alike. As employee expectations of job security wane, the alternative of temporary work becomes more attractive.

Getting Temporary Work

You can seek temporary work on your own—many employers advertise to fill temporary positions—or you can team up with a temporary help agency that will scope out temporary jobs and place you. You can have more confidence in the type of work you'll be expected to perform and the likelihood of receiving a paycheck if you work through an agency, an organization that knows your rights and ensures that you are treated fairly in your temporary position.

You can check your telephone book for temporary help agencies in your area, or search for temporary work on the Internet, either through temporary help agencies such as *www.net-temps.com,* or through job-search sites like *www. monster.com* or *www.hotjobs.com.* These are just a few examples; a quick Internet search will provide many more options.

If you don't want to use a temporary help agency, one of the best sources for temporary work is your former employer. If you leave a job on good terms you may be able to work out an arrangement whereby you continue to do some work for the company on a temporary or contract basis.

If you've never taken temporary work before, there are probably many questions you'll have regarding the nature of the work. Here are some answers to some of the more common questions:

What Skills Do You Need?

The type of work you apply for will dictate the skills you need. Many temporary positions are in the area of providing office assistance. Office workers are expected to possess basic typing skills and some computer skills as well. Many temporary help agencies provide training in these skills. For other jobs, consider what type of skills you would need if you were applying for the job full-time. The temporary help agency or a potential employer may ask you to take some tests so that it may assess your skills. Your prior work experience is an important facet of your skills package, and so are your basic personal presentation skills. You should be polite, well-spoken, and you should quickly grasp your place in the hierarchy of the workplace. You may have worked as a manager in a previous job, but if you're taking a lower-level position on a temporary basis, you may have to suppress your managerial tendencies.

How Many Hours Do You Need to Work?

Temporary work can be full-time or part-time, depending on the type of job and your aspirations. This is an issue you'll discuss with your potential employer or the temporary help agency you work with. You decide how many hours you are available to work—that is the beauty of temporary work. You can choose to not accept a job that doesn't meet your availability. Keep in mind that the fewer hours you are willing to work, the more limited your choices will be.

How Much Can You Expect to Earn?

The amount you earn depends on the type of job you take. You can assume the pay you receive will be less than what you would earn if you applied for the same job full-time. You are not in a strong negotiating position for most temporary jobs if there is a pool of other workers willing to take the job. On the other hand, the more skills you bring to the table and the more positive experiences you can demonstrate with previous employers, the more you are worth. You may find some negotiating room, considering that the employer does not need to provide you with benefits. If you are working through an agency, it will negotiate the best wage for you, but it will also take a cut for itself.

How Do You Get Paid?

Temporary workers are typically paid one or two weeks in arrears, depending on the agreement you have with the agency or your new employer. You work a week or two, turn in your hours, then your paycheck is processed in the next payroll cycle. If you work full-time through a temporary help agency you will probably qualify for holiday pay.

What Type of Temporary Work Is Available?

Today, there are jobs at all levels available for temporary workers. From directors to entry-level positions, companies hire temporary workers to augment the workforce. The more experience you have, the more opportunities are available to you. Gone are the days when temporary work was limited to "Kelly Girls" performing secretarial functions and answering the phone. Today's temporary workforce encompasses workers at all levels of age, skill, and value.

While many temporary jobs are still found in the clerical and general labor sectors, more companies are considering temporary workers for jobs in other types of occupations. The distribution of temporary employees by occupation as of 1998 showed the following breakdown of job types:

Administrative/clerical	35%
Operators, fabricators, laborers	31%
Precision production, craft and repair	7%
Service	7%
Technicians	5%
Professional supply	5%
Executive/managerial	5%
Marketing/sales	4%
Other	1%

Source: U.S. Bureau of Labor Statistics, 2000

Growth of temporary jobs in the years to come is expected to increase in all sectors, and particularly computer systems analysts, engineers, and scientists; marketing and sales occupations; operators, fabricators, and laborers; and precision production, craft, and repair occupations.

Employee vs. Independent Contractor

If you get a job through a temporary help agency, you most likely will be considered an employee of the agency. If you get a temporary job on your own, one of the things you will negotiate with the company you work for is whether you are to be considered an employee or an independent contractor. There are advantages and disadvantages to each in terms of what type of work you can be expected to do, how much control you have over how the job is done, when you do the work, and where you work.

Sometimes it's difficult to determine whether you are an employee or an independent contractor. However it's quite a difference as far as the Internal Revenue Service is concerned, because employers are required to withhold payroll taxes and pay Social Security, Medicare, and unemployment compensation, while business owners who hire contractors don't have that responsibility. Contractors, however, do have a responsibility to report their income on their tax returns and pay Social Security and Medicare tax on their own.

The IRS has published a list of twenty questions to help determine whether someone is a contractor or an employee, but the decision is not clear-cut. The general rule is that the more positive answers that can be given to these twenty questions by the person hiring you, the more likely it is that you are an employee rather than an independent contractor.

The IRS's Twenty Questions to Determine Employment Status

1. Do you (as the person paying the worker) give the worker instructions that he or she is expected to obey?
2. Does your company provide the worker with training?
3. Are the worker's services integrated into the regular business operation of your company?
4. Is it a requirement that the worker, personally, provide the services?
5. Is the worker prohibited from subcontracting the work?
6. Is the business relationship between your company and the worker an ongoing one?
7. Do you set the hours for the worker?
8. Is the worker expected to work full-time for your organization?
9. Is the work performed on your company's premises?
10. Do you instruct the worker regarding the order in which to perform his or her tasks?
11. Is the worker expected to submit reports (oral or written) that summarize his work progress?

12. Does the worker receive payments at regular intervals, such as weekly or monthly?

13. Does the worker get reimbursed for business and travel expenses?

14. Does your company supply the tools and supplies for this worker?

15. Does the worker have little or no significant investment in the tools used to perform the job?

16. Is the company responsible for absorbing any loss resulting from the work performed?

17. Is the worker prohibited from working for more than one company or person at a time?

18. Is the worker prohibited from making his or her services available to the general public?

19. Is it the company's responsibility if the worker does not perform to the specifications of the project?

20. Is the company responsible if the worker causes any damages?

Tips for Interviewing for Temporary Positions

Just because you are applying for a temporary position, don't think you don't have to make a good impression at the interview. You are still competing for the position. If you're going through a temporary help agency, you have to make a good impression there because the agency is screening people on behalf of the company where you will work. Then, if the potential employer also wants to talk to you, you have to make a good impression there, too. Whether you are going through an agency or finding opportunities on your own, you never know when a temporary position may alter the course of your career. Always prepare for *any* interview as if you are interviewing for the position of a lifetime. Here are some quick tips that may help you prepare for your interview. Some of these tips can be applied to both your interview with the temporary help agency and also to the company looking for help:

1. Learn about the company. Search the Internet for information about the company and read other sources of information that the company provides about itself. If you are referred to the company by a temporary help agency, ask the agency for background information on the company and any other advice for success on the interview.

2. Imagine yourself in the interview. Practice before going into the interview and try to anticipate the types of questions you will be asked.

3. Prepare questions for the employer. Your task in an interview is not just to answer questions, but also to ask some of your own. For example, you might ask about the employer's experience with and expectations of temporary workers, or you might ask about what potential there is for additional work beyond the term of the temporary position. Find out what you want to know so you can decide if you want the job.

4. Let the employer know you want the job. If you decide this is the job for you, let both the employer and, if applicable, the temporary placement agency know. Your enthusiasm for the job will be considered when the employer is choosing whom to hire.

Know Your Rights

You are not without rights as a temporary worker, and it is important when you take a temporary job that you understand those rights. It is also important that your employer understand your rights. If you work through a temporary help agency, you can feel relatively confident that everyone is on board with an understanding of the rights of the temporary worker. However, if you are striking out on your own, designing a temporary position with a former employer or through your own networking efforts, you need to be extra sensitive to the rights and protections you have under federal law. Among other things, you as a temporary worker have the following rights regarding these issues:

- **Harassment.** You have the right to not be the subject of gender or racial harassment. Harassment can include either spoken or written remarks, sexual advances, discrimination, physical or verbal misconduct, intimidation, and pranks.
- **Minimum wage and overtime pay.** You have the right to receive at least minimum wage for your work. If you work more than forty hours per week and are an hourly employee, you have the right to receive overtime pay, as defined by your employer. It is your responsibility to investigate the overtime pay policy before you accept the job.
- **A safe and healthy workplace.** You have the right to perform your duties as an employee in a safe and healthy workplace. As a temporary worker you have the right to receive the same safety equipment and company-provided precautions that are provided to permanent workers.

Creating Your Own Temporary Work

You don't have to rely on a temporary help agency to find work for you. If you are industrious and have some skills, you can create your own temporary work. If you like what you're doing, your temporary work may turn into a full-time, flourishing business venture.

First you must assess your own job skills. Start with an analysis of your background, your education, any on-the-job training you have received, and the type of work you have performed at previous jobs. List all the job skills at which you consider yourself to be qualified. Enlist the input of your family members and coworkers and listen to their depiction of your skills. You'll gain a lot of insight by hearing what others perceive as your strengths. Here is a path you should follow:

- **Choose a direction.** Consider all the items on your list, then focus on those job skills that you most enjoy performing and that you are best at. Think of how those skills can best be utilized in the workplace, what types of companies or other consumers are most likely to pay you for your skills, and how you can go about marketing your skills.
- **Hone your skills.** If you need to improve some of your skills in order to make them more marketable, consider additional education or even look for temporary employment in the areas in which you wish to improve.
- **Work with others.** When contemplating working on your own, you don't have to be a complete loner. Consider teaming up with someone you know who has complementary skills. Use networking skills to contact former employers and coworkers who might be able to point work in your direction, put the word out that you are looking for work, and ask friends and family members to do the same.
- **Promote your business.** You can start your business venture with the contacts you already have, or you can advertise your business. Get business cards printed, and maybe some flyers. Depending on the type of business skills you

have to offer, you can consider some print advertising. Initially, you should expect your promotion spending to generate enough business to pay for itself and then some.

Home-Based Businesses

If you're tired of pinching pennies and have some time on your hands, consider making your time worthwhile with a home business. Plenty of businesses lend themselves to work out of the home, depending on your interests and skills. If you've got the ambition and are willing to put in some hard work, you can turn part of your home into a thriving business that could even completely take the place of a lost job or an abandoned career.

Here are some ideas of businesses that can be run from the home. None of these businesses requires particular education or skills. Instead, these businesses are most successful when the proprietor's main characteristic is determination.

Lawn and Yard Work

Use your own yard, if you have one, as a demonstration area for your ability to keep the lawn fertilized, green, and manicured with the edges trimmed, the shrubs pruned, and the flowers colorful and prolific.

THE FAMILY BUSINESS

If your children are old enough, they can help with your new business. One advantage of having your children work for you is that wages paid to your own children are not subject to Social Security and Medicare taxes, which is a great savings for the business owner.

Pet Care

Walk dogs, feed and water pets, watch over pets for working or vacationing neighbors. The cost of kennel care for larger animals is high, and smaller animals such as bunnies and birds frequently don't qualify for such care at all. You can offer to care for animals for neighbors who are invalids, who travel with their jobs, or who need to go out of town. Offer to charge less than the local kennel fees and remind pet owners their pets won't be subjected to fleas or illnesses if they can stay in their own homes. Before taking on the responsibility of pet care, be sure to ask the person who hires you for emergency phone numbers for preferred veterinarians and the pet owners themselves so you can contact the appropriate people if an urgent situation needs attention while you're caring for the pet.

Day Care

Many parents who choose to stay home with their own children find they can better justify that decision by caring for the children of others as well. Suddenly the choice to be with children becomes a viable business that can be both financially and socially rewarding. You will need to consult the regulations in your state before starting a licensed day-care center.

Laundry Service

Full-time workers with busy schedules, invalids, neighbors who don't own washing machines or dryers, all appreciate having the option of having someone else do their laundry for them. Offer ironing and hanging services for an additional fee. If you're handy with needle and thread, you can include minor repairs along with your other service options.

Housecleaning

There are those people who leave the house all day, and there are those people who stay home and are able to keep up with housework. Housecleaning services proliferate, especially in big cities. Prepare a list of exactly what chores you're willing to do and get signed contracts before you embark on a housecleaning career. You probably want to get bonded as well to protect yourself from liability should someone accuse you of damage or theft while you're in a customer's home.

Tutoring

If you have a special skill in a particular aspect of school curriculum, and a way with children, consider using your talent to offer academic help to children in your local school district. Typically schools develop lists of approved tutors and distribute the lists to interested parents, so once you've developed a track record you can get recommendations directly from the school.

Word Processing

Are you a good typist and do you have a computer? Check the local paper or post ads on community bulletin boards for typing jobs.

Catering and Parties

Use your culinary talents to prepare food for parties. Expand your business to include invitations, decorations, music, and other entertainment. If you have children, hire the kids and their friends to serve food, park cars, replenish beverages, pass hors d'oeuvres, and so on. You can become a master at hosting parties for adults, teens, or small children.

Contemplating a Home-Based Business

You will need to consider many factors if you expect to operate your business from home. Foremost is the impact such a decision will have on your family. If you live with others, you must consider how your business will affect their lives, because it is their home too. Ask yourself these questions:

• Is there room in your home to operate your business? What happens if your business is successful and grows? You should plan for the future, not just for today.

• If you have children living at home, will they respect your need to segregate your work life from your home life? You must consider how having other family members nearby will impact working from your home.

• Can you work at home without being distracted by telephone, chores, family members, neighbors, television, a comfortable bed, errands, and so on?

• If you are considering a business such as a day care, or a business where clients visit you at your office, are you prepared for the impact of bringing others, perhaps strangers, into your home?

• Will you be able to quit work when the workday ends, or will you feel inclined to work around the clock, since you don't have the physical experience of leaving the company at the end of the workday?

Once you've reached a comfort level with all of these issues, and you're ready to proceed with a home business, you can consider the tax aspects of a home-based business.

The IRS and Your Home-Based Business

The IRS has had plenty of experience dealing with entrepreneurs who work from home. Your income from your business gets reported on your federal income tax return on Schedule C, Profit or Loss from Business. Expenses related to your job, such as advertising, automobile expense, insurance, legal fees, supplies, repairs, and travel and meals reduce your taxable income from the business and are also reported on Schedule C.

If you use your home for business, you are allowed to take a tax deduction for the portion of your home that qualifies as a business expense. The area you use for your home business must be used exclusively and on a regular basis for business. Exclusive use of your office space for business means the space can't do double duty: It's either business space or it's personal space. If the space is used for both business and personal, the IRS considers it all to be personal space.

Regular business use of the space means there needs to be an ongoing business use of the space. If, for example, you have an empty room that you used once to create a work of art, but the rest of the time you do your sculpting in your sunny studio, the empty room does not qualify as a home business space even though its only use was for business.

In addition to the regular and exclusive tests, the IRS has specific rules about what you can do in your home if you're going to call it a place of business. There are three rules that qualify your home business space for a deduction, but you need to meet *only one of them:*

- The area must be the principal place where you carry on your business.
- The area must be used as a place where patients,

clients, or customers meet with you in the normal course of your business.

- The area must be used in connection with your business (although not necessarily where you conduct business or meet clients) and is a structure separate from your home (a shed or warehouse used to store inventory, for example).

The home business deduction is reasonably straightforward if you conduct a business solely from your home and have an area set up exclusively for your business. You can share your business space with regular household activities, as long as you conduct only business in the business area of the house. For example, you might set up a desk in the laundry room and do your work there. You don't have to hang a curtain to separate the two areas—just don't fold laundry on your desk, and keep your business papers off the washing machine.

Recent changes to the tax laws permit a person to use a portion of the home as a home office or home business if there is no other space available for performing administrative duties, even if the person performs much of the job away from the home office. The example used by tax authorities to illustrate this situation is an anesthesiologist who performs medical work at several different hospitals, but uses his or her home office for billing, research, and scheduling because he or she has no other place to perform these duties.

If you qualify for a home office deduction, you are allowed to deduct a proportionate share of expenses such as mortgage interest, real estate taxes, homeowner's insurance, utilities, and maintenance (such as trash removal and septic service). You can also take a deduction for a proportionate share of repairs, such as roof repair, that affect the entire home.

206 SURVIVING FINANCIAL DOWNSIZING

When you fill out your tax forms, you will fill out Form 8829, Expenses for Business Use of Your Home. The expenses on this form will flow through to the form on which you report your business income (Schedule C, for example, if you are self-employed). Form 8829 asks for the square footage of the space used for your home business and the square footage of your entire home. If you can't figure out the square footage, you can enter the number of rooms used for your home business and the total number of rooms in your house or apartment. The percentage that results from dividing your business space by the space of the entire home is the percentage that will be applied to your home expenses for the purpose of calculating your deduction. Applicable expenses include mortgage payments, property taxes, rent, home-owner's or renter's insurance, repairs, and utilities.

One particular point to remember is that if you claim a deduction for the business use of a home that you own, you must take a deduction for depreciation expense on the portion of the home being used for business. This generates a nice deduction in the years in which you operate the business, but taking this deduction may result in a taxable gain when you sell the house.

One more rule: You can't claim a deduction for business use of your home to the extent that that deduction gives you a loss for your business. The exception to that rule is that home expenses that would normally be allowed as itemized deductions, such as mortgage interest and property taxes, are still allowed, even if the business activity results in a loss. Unused home business expenses can be carried over to next year's tax return.

Your choice to seek temporary work may be a short-range decision, or you may decide you prefer the freedom and flexibility of temporary work and plan to continue such a lifestyle for a long term. In either case, your search for temporary work can lead either to a long-term position with the company that hires you, or to references and connections for future employment. Look at temporary work as an opportunity and a chance to expand your skills and associations.

Chapter 12

Relocating to a New Home

SOMETIMES FINANCIAL DOWNSIZING results in small changes in your life: a more frugal shopping budget, an extension of credit on your credit cards, borrowing from family members, and so on. At other times a larger change must be made. While most of this book has focused on methods for downsizing that don't compromise your lifestyle, in this chapter we talk about a major change—a move to a new home.

The relocation may already be part of your downsizing plan. For example, often people who retire on a fixed income plan on moving to a smaller house, a retirement village, or an apartment. In other circumstances, a relocation may be an unexpected necessity. In either case, there are steps you can take that will make your relocation easy and efficient.

Cost Factors in Making the Decision to Move

There's a lot to consider when making the decision to move, but cost is one of the most important factors when deciding if it makes sense to relocate, particularly if you find yourself on a tighter budget.

A List for Moving

When you first consider moving, make a list of all the things that characterize your current home. Include the following types of items on your list, leaving out those that do not apply to you and adding more to suit your situation:

Cost:

- Monthly rent or mortgage
- Utilities: gas, electric, water, sewer
- Homeowner association fee
- Repairs (average)
- Cost of your commute to work (public transportation cost or number of miles)

House:

- Number of bedrooms
- List of other rooms
- Description of yard or other outside play area/garden
- Storage space
- Special design features

Location and Amenities:

- Local school
- Proximity to job
- Proximity to necessary shopping such as groceries, pharmacy
- Proximity to friends and family
- Pets
- Proximity to favorite entertainment such as theaters, malls, athletic facilities

Add other things to your list that are important to you and your family. Make your list as complete as possible.

Analysis of Your Moving List

When your list is complete, prioritize the noncost items on your list in their order of importance to you and your family. Is it desirable to stay in the same school district? Do you still require the same number of bedrooms or other rooms in your house? Do you have/want a garden? Does your home need to accommodate pets? Analyze each item on your list in terms of its significance in your lifestyle. Add items to your list that you would like to have in a home that you don't have now.

Consider the overall savings you wish to achieve by downsizing. For example, if your total monthly costs are now $1,200 and you can afford only $800 per month for all costs, note that you want to save $400 per month. Then go through the cost section of your list item by item, noting how much you currently spend on these items and estimating what these items will cost if you move to a new location.

Then, try to affix a cost to other items on your list. For example, if you want your children to attend the same school but need to move out of the district, how much will it cost in tuition and commuting to get them to their old school? If you rent, how much extra do you pay for a yard, extra bedrooms, and so on? Will you have enough storage space if you move or will you need to rent additional storage space? Are you currently able to walk to amenities like a grocery store, a pharmacy, a dry cleaner? When you consider moving think about the cost of getting to stores on a regular basis.

Requirements of Your New Home

Now that you've made a determination of how much money you need to save each month on your housing, it's time to figure out how to save that money without significantly changing your life.

Start by noting the items on your list that you can change or do without. Are you downsizing your family and thus can get by with less space? Are you ready to give up yard work in favor of moving into a condominium or an apartment complex? Can you find a new home with more efficient utilities, either by modernizing or moving to a more temperate climate? Make notes on your list, discussing the items with your family, so that you end up with an annotated list of the items of the highest importance to you and your family members.

Moving to a New Home

Aside from the emotional cost, there is a definite monetary cost associated with a move to a new location. You can ease the cost burden of the move by employing some cost-cutting measures.

Selling Unwanted Items

There is a thriving marketplace on the lawns and in the garages of American households, particularly in the warm months of the year. Examine the items you no longer want to keep for prospects that would fetch some money in a yard sale. If there is enough merchandise, the items sold in your yard can go a long way toward paying for your move, or for other expenses of your household. You might even consider organizing a neighborhood or an all-apartment sale and sharing in the promotional costs which may draw more potential shoppers to your collection.

If you have children, get them involved by encouraging

them to sort through their belongings as well. Offer to share the proceeds of the sale with them if they weed out their unwanted toys, books, and outgrown clothes. A word of caution: Double-check everything your child decides to sell before it reaches the sales tables. Things your child may consider unnecessary or unwanted may be items you want the child to keep, or family heirlooms you intend to store or pass on to other family members. Make sure you are involved in the pricing of the items the child intends to sell so you don't end up selling items for significantly less than their value. You may have spent $50 on a toy the child no longer wants, and while he or she may be happy to receive a couple of dollars for the item, it may be worth quite a bit more.

A fairly recent alternative to the yard sale is the online sale. If you have a computer and are willing to take the time to photograph and describe your unwanted items, you may find a ready market in the online auction arenas such as eBay (*www.ebay.com*), ubid (*www.ubid.com*), Yahoo auctions (*www.auction.yahoo.com*), and Amazon (*www.amazon.com*). Online auctions are easy to do out of your home and provide a ready audience of buyers looking for specific items.

Resale shops provide another outlet for selling unneeded items. Most towns have secondhand stores that either take items on consignment (where you leave the item and get payment if and when it sells) or else purchase items outright. You will probably make more money if you can find a consignment arrangement and if you have the time to wait while the item sits on the store shelves. But if you are in a hurry to unload things, take the cash upfront and be done with it. If you're hosting a yard sale and have items left at the end of the day, don't trudge back into the house with your arms loaded with unwanted items; fill up the back of the car and drive them over to a resale shop for some extra cash.

Donating Items to Charity

If you can't or don't want to sell your unwanted items, and the resale shop doesn't want them, keep on driving over to the nearest charity outlet, be it a Goodwill or Salvation Army type of store or a neighborhood church rummage sale. Hospitals are another source for taking and redistributing items to people in need.

No matter where you donate your items, keep in mind the possibility of taking a tax deduction for your donation. Although the tax deduction doesn't put money in your pocket today, you'll enjoy a benefit of lowered taxes next spring when you file your income tax return. If you itemize your deductions on your tax return, you can take a deduction for the resale value of the items you donate to charity. The deduction lowers your taxable income, which in turn lowers the taxes you pay.

For example, if you pay tax in the 15% tax bracket, a deduction worth $200 produces $30 worth of tax saving. It's really the same as taking your items to the IRS and exchanging them for $30 in cash, except you use a mid-dleman in the form of a charitable outlet and you have to wait until spring to get your money.

There are a few rules you want to follow if you are interested in claiming a tax deduction for donated items:

1. Keep a list of the items you donate. Don't just say "three boxes of clothes and other items" on your list; take the time to itemize your list to include descriptions like "7 men's shirts, 2 wool sweaters, 3 pair ladies shoes, 1 set of skis and poles, 24 hardcover books, 1 roasting pan" and so on. Not only does the list provide more evidence of your contribution, it is easier for you to value the items on a list than come up with an arbitrary amount for a box of unidentified items.

2. Get a receipt. The tax rules say you must have a receipt if the value of your items is $250 or more. The best rule is to just get a receipt no matter what the value is; in which case you'll always have evidence of your contribution. The receipt should indicate that items were received (the receipt doesn't have to include your itemized list), the date of the donation, the name and address of the charity, and a statement indicating that you gave the items with no strings attached and no expectation of getting anything in return for them.

3. Determine the value of the items you donated. This part can be tricky, because the quality of the items and the geographic location where you donate them affect the value. The best rule is to go to the store where they will be sold, or to a store in your area like a Goodwill store that sells similar items. Make a price list based on the items that appear in that store, listing how much typical items sell for. Then apply those prices to your list of donated items to come up with a fair value.

Here's a hint: If you are moving to a new location and the new location is a bigger city or the neighborhood is more upscale, go ahead and box up the items you intend to donate or sell, but take them with you and donate them or sell them at a resale shop at the new location. Resale items are usually worth more in higher-priced areas. In fact, if you live near an area that is more upscale, consider driving to that area and donating or selling your items in a more upscale neighborhood. If you are donating the items, make up your price list using the prices from the store that will sell the items. Be sure you get a receipt showing where the items were donated. Even if you donate the items to a church or other community center, you can still use the pricing structure at the nearby charity shops.

If you don't have a charity store near you and you want to donate items, check your phone book for charity services that pick up items, such as Goodwill, Salvation Army, veterans' groups, and churches. If your items are very worn, or if you donate in an impoverished area, value them at the lower end of the price range. If the items are like new, or if you donate them to a facility in an upscale area, use the higher end.

Packing and Moving

On the surface, a move may seem like a relatively straight-forward expense. You pay the movers, and—voilà!—you're located in a new home. But when you start taking apart all the small costs involved in a move, you'll find that there are many expenses to consider and they can really add up. Make a complete summary of all the costs of your move before you go, then try to consider making each cost as economical as possible. Some of your moving expenses are allowed as tax deductions, so be sure to read the section on tax considerations of a relocation in this chapter and think of the tax benefit as a reduction in your overall moving expenses.

Packing Yourself

There are two ways to pack: do it yourself or have someone else do it for you. If you're trying to watch your expenses, packing yourself is probably the most economical, as long as you pack tightly and take advantage of the opportunity to get rid of things you no longer need.

There is a time issue involved in packing yourself. If you hire someone to pack for you, the packers come to your house, pack everything, and do it quickly. If you pack yourself, you probably need more time in order to decide what things you want to pack and what you can part with, and also you may take the time to make decisions about how to pack effectively so that when you open the boxes at the other end of your move, your belongings will be easy to access and to put in their new places.

Another consideration in choosing whether to pack yourself or pay someone to pack for you is the issue of damage. Professional packers know how to pack items so they are not likely to break in the move. In addition, if something *does* break, the moving company takes the responsibility for damage to the item.

If you pack yourself, get good strong boxes that will hold your belongings. You can go to a moving company or to a self-move place like U-Haul to purchase official moving boxes. If you know someone else who is moving, consider splitting the cost of the boxes and using them for both moves. When the first person completes the move, turn the boxes over to the second person for reuse. Boxes sold by the moving companies are sturdy and can definitely hold up for multiple moves.

When you complete your move and the boxes are no longer needed, break them down and save them in an attic, basement, or other storage area and plan on using them again for your next move, or sell them at a yard sale and recoup a little of the money you spent on the move.

Hiring Packers

If you plan on hiring someone to pack for you, be it professional movers or even trusted friends, make the job easier by taking care of your weeding-out process in advance, emptying drawers, closets, and cabinets, folding and stacking items, stripping beds, and organizing all of your belongings in such a way that they can be packed quickly and easily.

Whether you pack yourself or have someone do it for you, be sure boxes are labeled, not just as to what room they go in at the other end of the move but with some general information about the box contents. That way you'll know which boxes you want to open first, and you can double check that the boxes are in the correct room before you open them.

Getting an Estimate

Moving companies are happy to provide estimates of the cost of a move. Call in advance and have a representative from the company come to your house to assess how much it will cost to pack and move you from one location to another. Get an estimate from more than one company so you can compare.

Moving companies provide different types of estimates, some are more binding than others, so be sure you know what type of estimate you are getting:

- **Binding estimate.** This is an actual estimate of the complete cost of the move, and the moving company is bound to stick by the estimate as its final price, assuming there are no changes in what has to be moved or where it is going between the time of the estimate and the time of the actual move.

- **Rate quote.** This is an estimate that provides a set rate for the time and mileage involved in the move. With a rate quote you don't have a fixed price for the entire job in advance of the move, but you know how much specific services will cost. Depending on how many hours are involved and how far it is between locations, your estimate may or may not be close to the actual bill.

- **Maximum bid.** This provides you with a ceiling on the cost of the move. The entire move will not cost more than amount quoted, and may cost less, but you will not know the specific fee until the move is completed.

Be sure to get any estimate from your moving company in writing. If you plan to sell or dispose of items before you move, do so before you get an estimate from the moving company. Alternatively, be sure to tell the movers which items aren't going with you when you move.

Consider moving in nonpeak times. Hiring movers during the summer or during traditional vacations can result in more expensive moving costs than if you move during a less busy time of the year.

Extra Charges the Movers May Assess

If you hire professional movers, be prepared for some unexpected charges. You should determine up front which if any of these charges may apply and what your moving company's policy is toward these types of expenses:

- **COD.** This isn't an extra charge but one you should anticipate. Most movers want to be paid when they deliver your belongings to the new location. You may even have to pay before the items are unloaded from the truck. Be prepared for the cost. Even if your employer is paying for the move, you may have to foot the bill up front, then get your reimbursement later.
- **Flight charge.** If movers have to walk up one or more flights of stairs, you may have to pay extra to have your movers move items up or down staircases.
- **Pick up and delivery charge.** If your items must be placed in temporary storage, you will incur extra expenses to

have the movers deliver to storage, then pick up the items and deliver to your new home. The storage cost is extra as well.

• **Extra mileage.** Road construction projects may interfere with your movers trying to travel in a direct route between your two locations. If the mover is rerouted from the original plan, you may have to pay extra for additional mileage.

Security Deposits

If you are a renter, don't forget to include your security deposit among your moving expenses. If you are vacating rented property, you should make arrangements to get your security deposit returned. Sometimes the security deposit serves as the last month's rent. If you have this type of agreement in place, talk to your landlord before the last month's rent is due and confirm that the landlord will hold the security deposit in lieu of your final rent payment. You can expect the landlord to want to inspect the property for damage before accepting your payment as final.

Renters should also expect to pay a deposit at the new location. Make sure you understand the terms for your deposit before making your payment. Will the security deposit be held in an interest-bearing account, and, if so, does the interest accrue to your benefit for the duration that the deposit is held? Will the deposit be used for your last month's rent? If possible, you should talk to other renters who have dealt with this landlord to find out the likelihood of getting your full deposit credited to you when you leave. Some landlords have a reputation for claiming there are damages in the amount of the deposit so that the renter is required to pay the final month's rent in addition to the deposit. Any arrangement you have for the disposition of the security deposit at the end of your lease term should be in writing and included with your signed lease agreement.

Moving Insurance

One of the expenses you should consider when adding up your moving expenses is the cost of insurance specific to the move. If you are moving yourself, check with the agent who provides your homeowner's insurance or renter's insurance to see what kind of coverage you have in place. If you are hiring movers, you can arrange for insurance through the moving company. There are three types of insurance to consider:

- **Limited liability insurance.** This type of insurance is included with the cost of your move when you hire professional movers, and is required by law. The coverage provides for a reimbursement of only 30 cents to 60 cents per pound if items are lost or damaged. If this is the only type of insurance coverage you have on the move, you probably will want to move your valuable items and heirlooms yourself.
- **Lump sum value insurance.** With this type of insurance you assign values to your possessions and your insurance premium is a percentage of the total value you insure. Typically you pay 1% of the insured value, so if you determine your possessions are worth $10,000, you will pay $100 for lump sum value insurance. With this type of insurance, the moving company will repair, replace, or reimburse you for lost or damaged items, based on the value you assigned prior to the move.
- **Full replacement value insurance.** This type of insurance provides for repair or replacement of lost or damaged

items based on their current market value. Check with your moving company for the cost of this type of insurance.

The Unexpected Costs of Selling a House

If you own your house you already know a lot about the extra costs that become part of the sale and purchase. Get out the realtor's closing statement from when you originally purchased your house to familiarize yourself with the types of expenses that a seller incurs, including a real estate agent's commission. If you use a realtor, your agent will inform you of all the costs you can expect.

One closing cost that homeowners are often surprised to encounter is the cost of unpaid real estate taxes. Real estate taxes are typically paid in arrears, and when you sell your home there may be one or more real estate payments that you have to make. These expenses relate to the taxes owing on the home when you owned it. You pay the taxes at closing so the new owner doesn't have to.

Tax Considerations of a Relocation

Some moves trigger a deduction on your tax return. If you qualify for a deduction for your move, you don't need to itemize your deductions to claim the tax break. Note that you must use Form 1040, as opposed to Form 1040A or Form 1040EZ to file your tax return if you plan to take advantage of the deduction for moving expenses.

Fill out Internal Revenue Service Form 3903, Moving Expenses, when you prepare your income tax return. On this form you will list all of the tax-deductible expenses associated with your move. This form gets attached to your federal income tax return for the year of your move. For more information about the tax effects of moving, you can request a copy of Form 3903, or you can request IRS Publication 521, Moving Expenses, by calling the IRS at 1-800-TAX-FORM (829-3676). You can also view these items online at *www.irs.gov.*

Here are the circumstances under which you can qualify for a deduction for moving expenses:

1. You must have a job at your new location. As an employee, you are required to work full-time for at least thirty-nine of the fifty-two weeks following your move. Your work doesn't have to be for the same employer, so if you leave one job and take another, you can still meet the thirty-nine-week requirement. If you are self-employed, the rule is that you must work full-time at least thirty-nine weeks out of the first fifty-two weeks following your move *and* you must work full-time for at least seventy-eight weeks of the first twenty-four months after your move. In other words, you must work seventy-eight weeks (eighteen months) of the first two years after you move, and thirty-nine weeks (nine months) of that work must occur in the first year after your move. Your self-employment doesn't have to be all the same type of work, but it must be full-time.

2. You have to pay for the moving expenses within one year of the move. There are exceptions to this rule, however. For example, if you move to take a job, and your family doesn't join you for eighteen months, you are still allowed to take the deduction for your family's moving expenses, assuming all the other rules are met.

3. You must meet the distance test associated with deductible moves. In order to qualify for the deduction, your new job must be at least fifty miles farther from your old home than your old job was from your old home. If this is your first job, the job must be at least fifty miles from your former home.

If your employer helps pay for your move, the employer is supposed to include the amount in your W-2 form at the end of the year. Your deduction offsets this amount that is reported as income.

Here are the moving expenses you are allowed to deduct on your federal income tax return.

- The cost of moving your household goods and personal effects. This expense includes packing services, the cost of boxes and other packing containers, and moving vans.
- The cost of connecting and disconnecting utilities.
- The cost of storing and insuring your household goods and personal effects for a period of up to thirty days *after* the items are moved to the new location and before they are moved to your new home.
- Your mileage for driving your vehicles one-way from your old home to your new home. As of 2004, mileage is deductible at a rate of 14 cents per mile. Alternatively you can deduct the actual cost of gas and oil for the vehicles if you keep accurate records for these amounts.
- The cost of lodging for yourself and your family en route from your old house to your new house. However, if you stop for visits, vacation, or sightseeing en route, that part of the travel and any related lodging is not deductible. Meals en route are not deductible, even if you travel for multiple days to get to the new location.
- The cost of shipping pets and vehicles to your new home.

If your employer pays for some of your move, you may be reimbursed for some expenses that are not allowed as a deduction. In that case, you may have some taxable income as a result of the moving expense reimbursement.

Individual states have different rules for what moving expenses are deductible. Check the rules for your state to see what expenses qualify as a tax deduction on your state income tax return.

Chapter 13

Enjoying the Time Off

AS WITH ANY OF life's events, approaching the loss of a job with a positive attitude can make the difference between merely surviving and actually benefiting from the experience. Whether by choice or through someone else's decision, you've found yourself with new time on your hands. Look at your time at home as an opportunity, a chance to regroup or a chance to enjoy the activities for which you now have time, and your positive attitude will make your time off among the best times of your life.

Quality and Quantity Time with Your Children

If you have children, your added time off will probably allow more time with them. There are many ways in which you can take advantage of this opportunity. Whether your children are young or older, rev up your parenting skills and make the most of an experience that can never be repeated. Your children will continue to grow and change and will eventually leave home. Use the time you have now to get to know them better and be a more prominent person in their lives.

Spend Time at Your Child's School

If your children are in school, you can use this opportunity to volunteer in their classroom, work on school projects and committees, get to know the other parents who are involved in school, or help out in the school administrative office. Your children will probably appreciate your giving some of your time to join and learn about the school activities, and you will be rewarded with better relationships and open lines of communication with school officials and other parents. You can also consider trying to get paying jobs either as a substitute teacher or an office helper to help pay the bills. If you want to participate in the schools in a bigger, more influential way, get involved with the school board or contact the school's administration offices to explore the possibilities of permanent positions.

Get Involved with One of Your Children's Activities

Work with the scouts, become an organizing parent for an athletic team, participate in parents' day out.

Help Your Child Start a Business

Since there may be more family focus on money these days, get your older child involved by helping the child choose and organize a small business venture in the neighborhood. Depending on the age of the child, the amount of responsibility the child is able to take, and the type of neighborhood in which you live, consider helping your child find a way to earn some spending money after school or on weekends by participating in any of a number of child-oriented jobs, including:

- Baby-sitting
- Mowing lawns
- Delivering newspapers
- Walking dogs
- Providing pet care for vacationers
- Picking up newspapers and mail for vacationers
- Running errands for elderly neighbors
- Doing housework
- Cleaning up and planting flowerbeds
- Raking leaves, shoveling snow
- Washing car interiors and exteriors
- Washing windows
- Bundling and selling kindling wood
- Painting houses
- Taking items to recycling center
- Sorting, tagging, and working at yard sales
- Cleaning out attics, garages, cellars
- Tutoring younger children

There are plenty of ways that an industrious child can earn some extra spending money, money for a car, or money to put toward college. A little imagination and some direction and guidance from a parent with extra time to help get the project off the ground can produce a child with a sense of responsibility and a child who learns what it's like to contribute to the family coffers.

Learn Together

Employ the principles of homeschooling by choosing a subject and immersing yourself and your child in the joy of learning something new together. Pick a subject that interests you both, then start with resources like the library and the Internet. Take field trips to museums or historic sites, if appropriate, to enhance your learning. If a field trip isn't an option, create your own imaginary trip and prepare brochures and a travel itinerary, just as if you were taking the real trip. If you're learning about a faraway place, find organizations in that location that can send material that will be useful to your learning experience. Use the Internet to communicate with people who can help with your learning.

Teach Your Child a New Skill

Use your extra time to hand down a practical legacy to your child, such as your knack for cooking or carpentry, your love for stamp collecting, your uncanny ability to balance the checkbook to the penny each month, your green thumb in the garden, or your gentle way with old folks. Find out what your child sees as his or her own special skills and reverse the learning experience by having your child show you some new skills as well, such as a flair on the dance floor, a love of animals, a special way of seeing the world through the lens of a camera, an aptitude for computers, or a talent for writing. Encourage your child to explore ways in which his or her skills can be used outside the home, either in part-time jobs or volunteer activities, participating in groups like 4-H, assisting teachers, or helping other students.

Read

Choose books you and your children enjoy and read together and to each other. Seek out other books by your favorite authors or books in the same style and expand your literary horizons.

Trace Your Roots

It costs only the price of a stamp to send letters to relatives asking for them to share their memories about childhood and their ancestors. Use this easy method to get a start on a genealogy study that you and your children will be able to hand down through the family. Use the computer to search for public records, take day trips to courthouses and cemeteries, get your family involved in learning about who all of you are and from where you originate.

Family Time

So far this chapter has focused on the additional time you can spend with your children. But you may not have children, and even if you do, your children are not necessarily the only members of your family, even though sometimes they may seem to be the most demanding.

You can also spend some of your newly found time with your spouse. If your spouse is employed, you may not be able to help with the work, but you can concentrate on improving the time the two of you share. The general topics mentioned in relation to improving time with children apply to a spouse as well. Learn new things together in your nonworking time, read together, learn new skills, and spend time doing the other things you enjoy together.

Our society has drifted away from the concept of the nuclear family where several generations live together and care for each other, but that doesn't mean you can't turn back the hands of time and focus your attention on other members of your family. You don't have to all live in the same household to learn from and give to one another, although living in the same household with other family members may be a viable alternative to your financial downsizing. You can consider pooling resources with other family members. If one family member works long hours and has a large house or family to maintain, you may be able to give of your new time to help care for that house or family in exchange for a temporary place to stay.

One cause for your need to tighten your family's finances may actually be directly related to your extended family. Perhaps your elderly relatives need care that you can provide by sharing your resources of time or money. If you don't have the extra financial resources to devote to other family members in need, you still may be able to give of your time to help with chores or other requirements of your extended family.

There may not be a need for you to help other family members, but you can use your time to improve relationships by simply corresponding, telephoning, e-mailing, or otherwise communicating more with other family members.

These are just a few suggestions to get you started on appreciating and enjoying your newfound time with your family. Depending on your interests, there are many more directions you can take that can help you make the most of the time you have with your loved ones. The rest of this chapter discusses suggestions for hobbies and projects you can enjoy during your free time. Whether you have free time by choice or you are between jobs and have only a limited time frame that you can share with your family, you can make the most of your time and create great memories, too.

Move Hobbies to the Front Burner

You may have a list in your mind of all the activities you've wanted to pursue but didn't have the time for while you were working. Those activities can now occupy your free time.

CATCHING UP ON ALL THOSE PROJECTS

Make a list of all the projects you want to complete, including the amount of time and the amount of money involved in each. Your list might include home repairs, renovation, cleaning the garage or cellar, sorting out old clothes, having a yard sale, acquiring and training a pet, or learning a computer program. Be sure to include some short-term projects that can be completed in a day or a few days, long-range projects involving planning and scheduling, and ongoing projects, such volunteering at school or the local hospital.

Hobbies can keep you busy and provide a sense of accomplishment while you search for another position or during a period of financial downsizing. You can even develop new skills that may become marketable while doing the things you enjoy most.

You can pursue plenty of hobbies from home with little or no additional expense. You can explore your dreams, even on a limited budget. Here are some examples:

- **Take a class.** Many community programs offer classes for a very small fee. Contact your local school for information about adult education classes, look for classes at craft stores or sporting centers, or consider taking music lessons.
- **Join a club.** Choose your area of interest, then find a group that's already organized, such as a reading group, a choir, a collector's club, a hiking club, a bible group, a political group, a community theater, a computer group, a parent/school co-op, or whatever suits you.
- **Learn a sport.** Find a local group that participates in a sport you want to learn, or recruit friends who want to

play. Investigate resale shops for the equipment you need. Consult with local coaches as to the best method for getting in shape and learning the sport.

- **Volunteer.** Choose an organization in which you believe and join as a volunteer.
- **Listen to music.** Visit the library, borrow from friends, or explore other ways of learning about and listening to music you enjoy.
- **Grow plants or flowers.** Seeds and small plants are inexpensive and rewarding to grow. Learn about the plants that proliferate in your region and get busy playing in the dirt!
- **Cook.** You'll kill two birds with one stone by indulging in a new hobby and cutting the food costs at home. Learn to cook economical meals that are nourishing and tasty.
- **Correspond.** Now's the time to catch up with friends and family or to write to someone you admire.
- **Be artistic.** Paint, make pots, draw, weave, find an outlet for that artistic interest of yours. Schools and community groups often offer adult training in these areas at little or no expense other than the cost of supplies.
- **Play games.** Find others with similar interests who want opponents for bridge games, euchre, chess, or other board or card games.

Vacations You Can Afford

If you have to cut your expenditures you probably believe you can't afford to take a vacation. If your definition of vacation is a trip to Disney World, travel abroad, renting a recreational vehicle, staying in hotels, or other equally expensive ventures, you're probably right.

But if your definition of vacation is spending time away from the day-to-day chores and concerns, focusing on yourself or your family, and relaxing, you don't need to run up the credit card balances to accomplish a wonderful and memorable vacation.

First, get your family together and have everyone participate in developing a definition of the perfect vacation. Make sure something from everyone's list is included in your bargain vacation.

Vacation with Friends

If vacationing on your own is too expensive, consider visiting friends or family members. Make the social time part of your vacation. Offer to plan and cook meals while you're visiting, and clean up after yourselves so you won't be an imposition. Do something special for your friends while you're there, like helping with a project they would normally hire someone for or put off entirely. Home projects seem like more fun when you can share them with someone else.

Alternatively, try planning to go somewhere with friends or family members. Taking others along to share the costs, add extra driving shifts, and take care of younger children, can make a vacation much more economical.

Another alternative to the traditional expensive vacation is a house swap. Find friends or family members willing to trade houses for a week or a few days. Pack your belongings just as you would for any family vacation, and move to another home. Eat meals out or purchase your own food to cook. Be sure to wash bed linens, make beds, and take out your trash before you return the home to its rightful owner (it's also a good idea to do these things in your own home before you turn it over to guests). You'll save on the cost of hotels and still get the advantage of visiting a new community.

Vacation at Home

You don't have to go somewhere to make your holiday seem festive. Try something simple like camping out in the back yard or on the living room floor. Or have everyone in the house swap bedrooms and pretend you're staying at a hotel. Don't just move down the hall and call it a vacation, pack clothes like you're actually going away and take them with you to your new room. Sleep late, stay up late, eat the kinds of snacks you'd have if you were away on vacation.

Promise yourself you'll cook meals that have never been tried in your family before. Find new recipes in your cookbooks, or go to the library and get cookbooks for food from some exotic locale. Do you dream of taking a holiday in Italy? Get a regional Italian cookbook and stock up on the ingredients for several days of Italian meals. Rent some movies that fit with the theme. While you're at the library get tour books and read all about the places you'd visit if you were actually overseas.

Be sure to act like a tourist in your own town while you're on vacation. Visit the local museums and other points of interest, or go to a sporting event. Take walking or driving tours, looking at the town as an outsider would.

Don't pick up the mail or answer the phone while you're on "vacation," so it will seem more like you're getting away from your everyday life. Send postcards to your friends and family. Just tell them you're taking a few days off from the regular pace of life and will call them when you return to your normal schedule.

Another alternative for a home vacation is to invite friends to visit you. Open your doors to people with whom you enjoy spending time, help your friends learn to appreciate your community while sharing meals, sleep schedules, and social events.

Dinner Parties and Day Trips

You don't have to devote several days to a special vacation. You can schedule just one day or an evening to share with your family or friends and let the memories last you for a long time into the future. Try planning a dinner party or luncheon with friends. You don't have to host a formal affair; just a casual cookout or hearty meal you prepare in your kitchen is enough to offer. You can cut costs on your party by throwing a pitch-in, instead. Invite a group and ask everyone to bring a dish—there will be plenty of food and you won't have to spend a lot of money.

Also consider taking short one-day vacations if you can't afford a lot of time off or a hotel room. Determine a reasonable radius around your house—maybe fifty or 100 miles, a distance you can easily drive in a couple of hours—and investigate alternatives for exploration. Maybe there's a town you've never seen, farms to visit, parks ripe for picnics, outdoor community concerts, historical courthouses, small-town diners, civic theater, train rides, unusual architecture. The possibilities are limited only by your interests and the available surrounding communities.

The Internet is an excellent source for quick vacation material, information about the towns and areas in your state, and reviews of restaurants. Your library can also provide state tour books and access to the Internet if you don't have a computer at home.

Renovating and Redecorating

Another alternative to going away is to make your home seem like a new place by renovating or redecorating. Try rearranging furniture, painting, shopping garage sales and flea markets for items that can dress up your surroundings. You don't have to hire a decorator or spend a fortune to make your home seem fresh and exciting. If you have enough rooms, consider trading bedrooms with another family member. You can enjoy redecorating your rooms without having to move to a new home.

Look at books and magazines for ideas, choose color schemes, and tackle one room at a time. Perform necessary repairs. If there is a handy person in your family, go to the home repair stores and take care of renovations yourself. Build shelves, acquire storage units, or simply sort out items to get rid of clutter and unwanted belongings.

Weed and replant yards with inexpensive seed packets. Dig up old planted items that no longer grow, or transplant items to make your garden look new. If you don't have a garden, consider pots for the porch or window boxes, or look into acquiring houseplants that are easy to maintain. You can find flower pots for a small price at yard sales, and decorate them to fit your home environment with inexpensive paints or decals.

Take before and after pictures so you can see your progress and remember how your home looked before you started making changes.

Conclusion: Surviving and Thriving

Financial downsizing doesn't have to mean personal downsizing. All aspects of your life combine to form an opportunity to add to your income and cut your expenses without significantly altering your lifestyle. With careful planning and a thorough understanding of the factors that contribute to your preferred way of living, you can survive financial downsizing while living the satisfying life you desire.

Index